JOHN
ADAMS

PRESIDENTIAL ✦ LEADERS

JOHN ADAMS

CAROL H. BEHRMAN

LERNER PUBLICATIONS COMPANY/MINNEAPOLIS

To Edward with love and appreciation for sharing his vast knowledge of history with me

Publisher's Note: John Adams, like many men and women of his time, did not always use conventional spellings or capitalizations in his writing. We have printed his words as he wrote them.

Lerner Publications Company
A division of Lerner Publishing Group
241 First Avenue North
Minneapolis, MN 55401 U.S.A.

Website address: www.lernerbooks.com

Library of Congress Cataloging-in-Publication Data

Behrman, Carol H.
    John Adams / by Carol H. Behrman.
        p.   cm. — (Presidential leaders)
    Summary: Profiles John Adams, an influential patriot during the American Revolution who became the nation's first vice president and second president.
    Includes bibliographical references and index.
    ISBN: 0–8225–0820–6 (lib. bdg. : alk. paper)
    1. Adams, John, 1735–1826—Juvenile literature. 2. Presidents—United States—Biography—Juvenile literature. [1. Adams, John, 1735–1826. 2. Presidents.] I. Title. II. Series.
E322.B44 2004
973.4'4'092—dc21   2002153398

Manufactured in the United States of America
1 2 3 4 5 6 – JR – 09 08 07 06 05 04

CONTENTS

❖

John Adams *did not shy away from doing what he believed
to be right, even if it was not a popular choice.*

INTRODUCTION

"One of the most gallant, generous . . . actions of my whole life and one of the best pieces of service I ever rendered my country."
—John Adams on his defense of British soldiers after the Boston Massacre

John Adams, who openly opposed British policies, was the talk of Boston, Massachusetts. Bostonians were shocked that the young patriot lawyer would appear in court to defend hated British soldiers. Most people in North America's British colonies, such as Massachusetts, had always thought of themselves as loyal subjects of King George III. In recent years, however, they had begun to question that loyalty, encouraged by patriots like Adams.

Colonists believed they were living with unfair laws and taxes. A final insult was the stationing of British soldiers in the streets of Boston. King George III was determined to bring the people of Boston into submission. The colonists responded with angry protests. Mobs gathered in the streets to taunt the soldiers. During one disorderly protest

on a cold night in March 1770, shots rang out. British soldiers had killed five colonists and had wounded six more.
This tragic event came to be known as the Boston
Massacre. It outraged and inflamed not only Bostonians
but also all thirteen American colonies.

When the British soldiers were brought to trial that
same month, they needed a defense attorney. John Adams
accepted the challenge, even though he was a leader among
the patriot groups. These patriots demanded that the
British government change their policies toward the
colonies. Adams's patriot friends warned him not to take on
such an unpopular case. They told him the public would
hate him. Any hopes he might have for a career in politics
would be doomed.

Adams was stubborn when it came to doing what he
believed was right. "Counsel [legal representation] ought to
be the very last thing that an accused Person should want
[lack] in a free country," he declared and went ahead with
the defense. All his life, this would be a hallmark of
Adams's character—to do what was right regardless of personal consequences. This insistence on justice and fairness
was one of his important contributions toward founding a
great nation.

CHAPTER ONE

THE BOY FROM BRAINTREE

"My father was the honestest Man I ever knew.
I have never seen his Superior."
—John Adams

John Adams was born on October 19, 1735, in the village of Braintree, Massachusetts, about ten miles from Boston. His father, John Adams Sr., was a farmer and a shoemaker. His great-great-grandfather, Henry Adams, had emigrated in 1638 from England and worked hard to establish a successful farm. The land was rich and produced excellent crops. Each succeeding generation acquired more land. By 1735 the Adams holdings included many acres of farmland and pastures. Young John was born in a small, two-story farmhouse that still stands. His father was a respected community leader. He was a selectman on the town board. This board of selectmen passed laws and made decisions necessary to govern the town. John Sr. was also a deacon, or leader, in the local Puritan congregation. The townspeople called him Deacon Adams. His wife, Susanna, was from the prominent Boylston family. The Adamses were not wealthy. Even a large farm such as theirs produced only enough to cover the basic needs of a growing family. They put in long hours of toil on the farm and in the home. There was only enough money to send one of their sons to college. John, the eldest, knew early on that his parents wanted him to attend nearby Harvard University and become a minister.

As a boy, John did not dwell on the future. His childhood was happy and carefree. Chores at home consisted of simple tasks, such as feeding the chickens and gathering dry

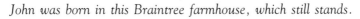

John was born in this Braintree farmhouse, which still stands.

twigs for the fireplace. He had plenty of free time to roam the hillsides and woods. He often walked to the nearby bays and inlets of the Atlantic Ocean to watch the fishing boats. John and his friends played games, such as hopscotch, marbles, tag, and badminton. The children flew kites and played ball games. Fishing and horseback riding were also popular. When he was nine, John learned to use a gun. Hunting became his favorite sport.

The Adams family, including John and his two younger brothers, were close. John adored his mother. He respected and admired his father, who preached the morality of the Puritan religion in his sermons at the meeting house. John accompanied Deacon Adams to town meetings. He saw democracy in action as citizens and their elected representatives tried to solve community problems. John was proud of his father's accomplishments. He later wrote, "Almost all the business of the town [was] managed by him for 20 years." John hoped he would grow up to be like his father—an honest, upright man, dedicated to the truth and to serving God and his community.

EARLY EDUCATION

At the age of five, John attended the local schoolhouse across the road from his home. A widow named Mrs. Belcher taught reading, writing, and arithmetic. *The New England Primer* was their text. It taught Puritan morality along with reading. The alphabet lesson for "A" was about the story of creation in the Christian Bible. It said, "In Adam's fall we sinned all." The children also read and recited Christian verses such as, "There is a dreadful fiery hell, where wicked ones must always dwell."

Dame Belcher was a kind, humorous woman. John, who was bright and quick witted, was one of her favorites. During the fall term, she carried corn from her farm to the mill. John was her assistant. She gave him three coppers (pennies) for his help, telling him that he must save his money and buy land with it. Like any young boy, however, John found better uses for the money, such as buying candy and colorful kites.

At ten, John left Dame Belcher's classroom for a school for older boys. His father enrolled him in the Braintree Latin school. Here he would prepare for the entrance examinations needed to enroll in Harvard University. Joseph Cleverly, a Harvard graduate himself, was the schoolmaster. He was an intelligent man but a lazy, boring teacher. John hated school. He skipped it whenever he could, running off to fish or hunt. He informed his father that he did not want to go to college but preferred to become a farmer. Deacon Adams nodded. "I will show you what it is to be a farmer," he told his son. "You shall go with me to Penny Ferry tomorrow morning and help me get thatch [straw]."

The following day, John worked with his father all day, up to their knees in mud, cutting and tying thick bundles of thatching. It was exhausting work. At the end of the day, Deacon Adams asked John how he liked being a farmer. The boy's muscles were sore and he ached all over, but he was stubborn. He told his father, "Sir, I like it very well."

"Aye," his father said, "but I don't like it so well, so you shall go to school."

Latin school did not get any better. When he was fifteen, John told his father that the real reason he hated school was because of the teacher. Deacon Adams agreed to send John to Joseph Marsh, who ran a private boarding school nearby. In return, John promised that he would work harder in school. Marsh proved to be a wonderful teacher. John performed brilliantly under his patient instruction. He also began to appreciate books and learning.

JOHN GOES TO HARVARD

In less than two years, Marsh felt that John was ready to take the entrance exam for Harvard. John himself had doubts about his own abilities. He suffered pangs of anxiety during the journey to Harvard. Despite these fears, John passed the exam and was admitted to Harvard, where he began his studies at the age of sixteen.

At Harvard his appetite for knowledge grew by leaps and bounds. It was the first time he had lived among

---

Established in 1636, Harvard was modeled after British universities. In the early years of the school, many ministers were educated there.

scholars, philosophers, and political and social activists. He became aware that a deep curiosity about all things was growing within him, together with a love for books and study. Great issues of the past and present were endlessly discussed. John flourished in this environment. He showed skill at speaking in front of groups. Friends advised him to study law instead of becoming a minister. John had always supposed he would go along with his parents' wish for him to enter the ministry. But he was beginning to believe that he would be more suited to the law. John didn't feel ready to make a choice immediately. He decided that he would teach school after graduating while trying to make up his mind about a future career.

One of the guests at the Harvard graduation ceremonies of 1755 was Thaddeus Maccarty from the town of Worcester, Massachusetts. He was looking for a new schoolmaster for his town and was impressed by the eloquent speech made by a graduate named John Adams. Maccarty offered the position to John, who accepted immediately.

CHAPTER TWO

JOHN ADAMS, ESQUIRE

*"Lawyers in Worcester are one thing, but have
you any notion, Adams, what the province
at large thinks of the profession?
We are hated, mistrusted."*

—James Putnam, Worcester lawyer

Worcester, fifty miles from Boston, was larger than
Braintree. Compared to the intellectual atmosphere of
Harvard, however, the new schoolmaster at first found it
dull and dry. "Hope has left me," John wrote to a friend.

The school was a one-room log house facing the Worcester
town green (central park). John taught a dozen boys and girls
of different ages. Classes lasted from early morning until
evening. John wanted to be a good teacher, not like the awful
Mr. Cleverly. He tried to be sympathetic to his pupils and
inspire them with a love of learning. He believed that "human
nature is more easily...governed by...encouragement and praise
than by punishment and...blame."

His students were not as responsive as he would have wished. He complained about the "large number of little runtlings, just capable of lisping ABC, and troubling the master." Sometimes he was thrilled by a student's success. Other times he groaned about "the mischievous tricks . . . and the stupid dulness of my scholars." He found the job to be exhausting. It drained all his energy. His duties gave him little time for study and self-improvement.

In Worcester John began a diary in which he inscribed his thoughts, feelings, and ideas about every detail of his life and the world in which he lived. He kept this diary for

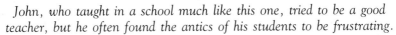

John, who taught in a school much like this one, tried to be a good teacher, but he often found the antics of his students to be frustrating.

thirty years. It provides a mirror to the times in which he lived and to his own growth and development. His entries show the high goals he wanted to achieve. They describe the pain he felt when faced with his own shortcomings.

To meet his many goals for self-improvement, John set a challenging schedule for himself. "I am resolved to rise with the Sun," he wrote. "I will . . . think upon what I read and what I see. I will strive with all my soul to be something more than Persons who have had less Advantages than myself." But the next day he lazed in bed and wrote sadly in his diary, "This is the usual fate of my resolutions."

Like most young people trying to find their way in the world, he was nagged by self-doubt. He found it difficult to control his thoughts and wishes. "My Brains seem constantly in . . . great Confusion and wild disorder." Nevertheless, he made time for reading and studying. His favorite subjects were Latin and history.

CHOOSING A PROFESSION

The twenty-year-old schoolmaster from Harvard also made time for socializing. John was happy to be invited into the social life of Worcester. He discovered a circle of friends with whom he felt comfortable. With them he could discuss the great thoughts and questions that appeared in the books he studied. Most of these friends were a bit older, but they encouraged John to speak out and express his opinions freely.

One close companion was a lawyer in his late twenties named James Putnam. Putnam was impressed with the younger man's intelligence and quick wit. He urged John to become a lawyer, but John still had doubts about a choice of career. He worried that he lacked the wealth or family connections to rise in the field of law, "not to mention capacity [ability] which I have not."

Putnam began to take John to sessions of the Court of Common Pleas, where disputes between ordinary people were resolved. John was fascinated by the variety of interesting cases he saw there. Afterward, the two friends would have lively discussions about the proceedings. This sparked John's interest. He finally decided that the law was a noble calling. Despite its many "difficulties and discouragements," he was now "irresistibly" compelled to follow it.

Most colonists interested in the legal profession prepared for the law exam by studying with a licensed attorney. James Putnam offered to perform this service, and John eagerly accepted. On August 22, 1756, he wrote in his diary, "Yesterday I compleated a Contract with Mr. Putnam, to study Law under his Inspection for two years." John also added his deep moral convictions. He promised himself never to commit any meanness or injustice in the practice of law.

John had saved enough money for Putnam's fee of one hundred dollars. He still needed funds for housing and food but did not want to ask his father for help. He felt it was time for him to be independent. Instead, he supported himself by continuing to teach for two more years during his period of apprenticeship. It was a grueling schedule. John had no time for the dreaming and time wasting he despised, and he made fewer reproachful entries in his diary.

John's apprenticeship with Putnam ended in the late

summer of 1758. He did not want to compete with his teacher in Worcester. There was no attorney in John's hometown of Braintree, so he returned home to live with his parents and to practice law. The residents of Braintree had a reputation for bringing frequent lawsuits, so John could expect many clients. "The village has become so petty quarrelsome," he noted in his diary, that the townspeople had earned a reputation for going to court often.

BACK TO BRAINTREE

First, Adams had to go to Boston and find a sponsor in order to be allowed to practice law in Massachusetts. He felt inadequate among the well-known, impressive attorneys there. The lack of family connections troubled him. He had no influential relatives in Boston who could help advance his career. "It is my destiny," he told his diary, "to dig treasures with my own fingers." He asked several prominent Boston lawyers to sponsor him. They questioned the young man closely and were impressed by his knowledge and ability. On November 6, 1758, the colony of Massachusetts granted twenty-three-year-old John Adams permission to practice law. He returned to Braintree to begin his career.

The new lawyer did not get off to a good start. His first case involved a dispute over a horse, and he lost it on a technicality. The client was angry and cursed Adams loudly. "It will be said, I don't understand my Business," Adams worried. He was fearful that no one would want him again. Fortunately, he won many of the cases that followed.

His career was soon on its way, and Adams was able to spare time to enjoy a social life with other young men and women of Braintree. His circle included a wide variety of people from all walks of life. People found him amiable and a sparkling conversationalist, though sometimes a bit over-bearing. He was so widely read that he could talk about almost any subject. He sometimes tended to go on at length and fly off in a hundred different directions when he was passionate about a topic. But his information was always accurate. Adams and his friends engaged in endless discussions but also enjoyed sing-alongs and playing cards. As usual, too much enjoyment brought self-criticism in his diary. "Laziness, languor, inattention, are my bane," he complained, and "my mind is liable to be called off from law by a girl, a pipe . . . a play."

FIRST LOVE

John Adams was not a handsome man. He was short and somewhat pudgy, but his humor and clever conversation made him popular even among the ladies. There was one young woman in particular who attracted him. Her name was Hannah Quincy, and he sought her company often. She was beautiful, popular, and flirtatious. Adams was charmed. He fell in love for the first time and thought Hannah might return his feelings.

It was a shock when his best friend, Richard Cranch, brought the news that Hannah was marrying another man. Adams was devastated. He could not get Hannah off his mind. Instead of focusing on his work, he found himself dreaming of her face and friendly smile.

Adams tried to forget Hannah by throwing himself

with greater intensity into his law practice. For the next few years, the young lawyer could only practice in the colony's inferior, or lower, courts. But his superiors noticed the brilliant work Adams did in these lower courts and rewarded him. In 1761, at the age of twenty-six, he was sworn in as a barrister (a higher-level lawyer) of the Superior Court of Massachusetts. As a barrister, he would wear a black gown and powdered wig to court. The promotion gave John the opportunity to go into Boston several times a week and to take more interesting cases there and in outlying areas.

This success was marred by the death of his father several months earlier. Both of Adams's parents had fallen ill during a severe epidemic of a contagious disease called influenza. His mother recovered, but Deacon Adams died. It had been a great blow to Adams. His father had been his hero, the man he most wanted to be like. With enormous sorrow, Adams himself wrote Deacon Adams's obituary, calling him "a man of strict piety and great integrity, much esteemed and beloved wherever he was known."

ABIGAIL

During this same period, Adams accompanied Richard Cranch on a journey to the nearby town of Weymouth. Richard was courting the eldest daughter of the Reverend William Smith, who lived in the town. John Adams became enchanted with Smith's younger daughter, Abigail. He had met Abigail two years earlier, but she had still been a girl. Since then she had grown into a lovely young lady.

Abigail was quite unlike the other women Adams had met. She was direct and unaffected. She did not engage in

Abigail grew up in this house in Weymouth.

coy flirtations and was not afraid to show her intelligence. She was always ready to speak her mind and not at all backward about expressing thoughts and opinions on all subjects. In other words, she was very much like Adams— his counterpart in a female. Soon Adams was finding more and more "business" that made it necessary for him to travel to Weymouth. It didn't take long for Adams and Abigail to realize that they were destined for each other.

CHAPTER THREE

HUSBAND, FATHER, ACTIVIST

"You . . . have always softened and warmed my heart . . . You shall polish my sentiments . . . and . . . banish all [my] unsocial and illnatured particles."
—John Adams to Abigail Smith

Abigail Smith was seventeen when John Adams began courting her. She was petite and slim, with sparkling dark brown eyes. Her father, William Smith, was the minister of Weymouth. Abigail was a dutiful daughter. She worked diligently at mastering all the skills expected of women. These included making soap and candles, milking cows, spinning and weaving, and even preparing medicines.

Most girls did not attend school at that time, but Abigail's father noticed that she had a quick mind. He encouraged her to educate herself at home by reading

Abigail Adams as a young woman

——— ✧ ———

books. When not busy with her chores, Abigail Smith could always be found in her father's large library, reading and learning. She was developing opinions on every subject under the sun.

John Adams was twenty-six. He had a fair income from his law practice and had inherited the family farm and a house from his father. He was well educated and had an active mind. Adams still had many self-doubts and constantly questioned his worthiness. But he had enough confidence to express his opinions with determination and strength. Sometimes he was too quick to point out to other people ways in which they might improve themselves. Folks who did not know Adams may have been put off by this tendency. To his large and growing circle of friends, it was just an amusing and quirky part of Adams's personality.

The brilliant lawyer did not intimidate Abigail Smith. Others sometimes found him stiff and pompous. She saw a kind, sensitive, passionate young man. She stood up to him in every discussion with a gentle strength of will and matched his arguments point by point. Most young men would have been put off by such feistiness in a girl. But Adams found it incredibly attractive. He liked arguing with

Abigail. In fact, he liked everything about her. He began visiting Weymouth as often as possible, and before long, they were deeply in love. When they had to be apart for even a brief time, letters flew back and forth. He called her "Miss Adorable."

"O my dear Girl," he wrote during one absence, "I thank Heaven that another Fortnight [two weeks] will restore you to me." In another letter, which he delivered himself, he demanded that she "give [the bearer] as many kisses . . . as he shall please to Demand and charge them to my Account."

When Adams was in Boston for many weeks, Abigail wrote to him every day. She begged him to follow the doctor's instructions and to guard his health "upon which depends the happiness of your A Smith."

One time Abigail asked Adams for a list of her faults. Adams was always ready to improve himself and others, even his beloved. He sent her a list of six items. These included poor card playing, singing, not sitting up straight, and even "sitting with the Leggs across [crossed]." Abigail acidly pointed out that "a gentleman has no business to concern himself about the legs of a lady."

The courtship went on for several years. The couple became best friends, as well as sweethearts. Adams lovingly listed Abigail's virtues in his diary. "Tender, feeling, sensible, friendly, a friend . . . Not a disagreeable word or action . . . Prudent, modest, delicate, soft, sensible."

MARRIAGE AND FAMILY

On October 25, 1764, the couple was married in Abigail's father's home. Afterward, they moved into the farmhouse

Adams had inherited from his father. Adams was twenty-nine and Abigail nineteen. The following July, their first child was born. It was a girl whom they named Abigail. They called her Nabby. Two years later, Abigail gave birth to their second child, John Quincy.

All was well in the Adams household. Adams's law practice was flourishing. By 1768 he had become one of the busiest lawyers in Boston. Adams and Abigail were content in their personal life. But outside the cozy home in Braintree, events were occurring that would lead to a great upheaval in their world.

BRITAIN AND ITS AMERICAN COLONIES

While John Adams was establishing a new home with Abigail, Great Britain was having difficulties with its American colonies. Most of the colonists were of British origin. They had been loyal subjects of the king. But cracks in the relationship between the colonies and Britain had begun to appear.

After decades of settlement and growth, the people of the American colonies had become markedly different from their British cousins. Britain had a stable society built on centuries of tradition. Americans were more open and free. British men and women were born into rigid social classes. It was almost impossible for anyone to rise above his or her class. In the American colonies, opportunities were often limited only by one's skills, willingness to work, and sense of adventure. American colonists developed self-reliance and independence. But many people in Britain thought the colonists were inferior, without culture or ability.

In 1754 Great Britain had engaged in a costly war

against the French and certain Indian nations in North America. Colonists had fought alongside their British brothers in that conflict, since much of it took place on American soil. Their aim had been to protect British-controlled land from the French and their Indian allies.

In 1763 the British won the war against the French and the Indians. The British Parliament, which included no representatives from the colonies, decided that the American colonies should help pay for the cost of that war. With the approval of the king, a Stamp Act was imposed on the colonists. This new law required that every newspaper, pamphlet, business document, and legal paper carry a stamp.

The colonists were outraged by this new tax. The Stamp Act had been passed without their consent or participation.

─────────────── ✧ ───────────────

Colonists were supposed to make sure that stamps such as these were on important documents.

Samuel Adams was a Boston businessman who became involved in politics.

◇ —————————

They said it was "taxation without representation." Spokesmen for the colonists petitioned the British government to repeal, or abandon, the Stamp Act, but their petitions were ignored. Angry and frustrated, some of them formed a group in Boston. They called themselves the Sons of Liberty. John Adams's cousin, Samuel Adams, was their leader. The Sons of Liberty held loud protests in the streets. They pressured merchants to boycott, or avoid buying, British goods. Soon Americans were divided into two factions. The patriots believed in fighting for the right of the colonists to refuse to pay taxes without a voice in Parliament. Loyalists supported the policies of the British government.

John Adams agreed with the patriots. He believed that the Stamp Act went against British law. Unlike his cousin, Samuel, he was opposed to force and wanted to achieve a peaceful solution. As the king continued to ignore the pleas of the colonists, John Adams agonized over the right course for the colonies to follow. He was a person of influence in Boston. He knew his thoughts and recommendations would be taken seriously.

Adams studied and discussed the problem endlessly in conversations with other colonists and in his writings. He wrote a convincing essay that appeared in a newspaper called the *Boston Gazette.* This article examined the Stamp Act from every legal point of view. It concluded that the acts of the king and Parliament were illegal and that the British government was misusing its power.

Despite colonial opposition, the British government insisted on enforcing the Stamp Act. In Boston the people were so angered by the new law that the British didn't dare bring the stamps into the city. Fearful of riots, they kept the stamps on an island in Boston Harbor. Still, King George III was determined to force the colonists to submit. This made John Adams more and more active in the pursuit of rights for the colonists. "The Year 1765," he wrote in his diary, "has been the most remarkable Year of my Life. That enormous Engine fabricated by the british Parliament, for battering down all the Rights and Liberties of America, . . . has raised and spread, thro the whole Continent . . . a spirit that will be recorded to our honor with all future generations."

Adams drew up a set of resolutions, or statements of purpose, opposing the Stamp Act. He hoped that a clear explanation of why it was illegal would influence the thinking of people in the colonies as well as in Britain. He based his opinion on British law. The colonists did not have to pay the tax, he argued, because they had no representation in Parliament and had not consented to this law. Adams's

Colonists in Boston and other cities resisted paying the taxes imposed by the Stamp Act. Some Bostonians were so angry that they rioted.

defense of the patriots' cause brought him great popularity. He was elected a selectman for the town of Braintree. He had not even campaigned for the office, and he was pleased by the approval of his neighbors. He was determined to serve the people well.

Unfortunately, the arguments that Adams and others had made against the Stamp Act did nothing to change the minds of Parliament and the king. For their part, the colonies refused to comply with the Stamp Act. Feelings against the home country ran high, especially in Boston. The Sons of Liberty strengthened their protests and their pressures on fellow colonists to resist the tax. British merchants were feeling the strain. Finally, on March 18, 1766,

Parliament repealed the Stamp Act. The colonists were jubi-
lant. "Bells rung, Cannons were fired, Drums beaten,"
Adams recorded in his diary.

Adams's only disappointment was that the town of
Braintree did not give him as much appreciation as he
thought he deserved. He believed he had been a vocal and
active leader of the faction that succeeded in getting the
hated tax repealed. "I had the mortification to see that
while allmost all the . . . opposers of the Stamp Act [were
honored] by their towns," he complained, but "I was . . .
neglected." Although he had been elected a selectman of
Braintree, he still felt unappreciated. It seemed to him that
others who had done less had received more recognition.

CHAPTER FOUR

RUMBLINGS IN THE COLONIES

"My heart bled for the poor people of Boston."
—John Adams

The Stamp Act marked a major change in the way many colonists felt about their relationship with Great Britain. A desire for liberty had begun to burn in the hearts of many of them. They wanted respect and participation in government. But King George III stubbornly refused to recognize any of the changes they were seeking.

John Adams was one of those who had been stirred by ideas of freedom. After the repeal of the Stamp Act, some peace and calm returned to the colonies. But the new questioning spirit continued to flower. In parlors and taverns, people met to talk about the relationship between citizens and their government. They discussed new ideas such as a person's natural right to individual freedom.

Even though many colonists desired change, King George III consistently denied their wishes.

——————————— ✧

They wondered what they could do if governments denied them these important rights.

THE ADAMS FAMILY MOVES TO BOSTON

John Adams's law practice was doing well. But the cases he worked on required him to spend more and more time in Boston. He didn't like being away from Abigail and the children. However, there was much more excitement and stimulation in Boston. The larger city also offered greater financial opportunities. In 1768 Adams decided to move his family to a house in Boston. In December Abigail gave birth to their third child, Susanna. Sadly, Susanna died before the age of two.

Boston was a beehive of activity compared to quaint Braintree. More than eighteen thousand people lived there. The crowded streets bustled. Boston had also become the center of patriot unrest. Adams was right in

In the mid-1700s, Boston was a lively colonial trade center.

———————————— ✧ ————————————

the thick of it. Soon the Adams home saw a steady stream of visitors. These often included Adams's hotheaded cousin, Samuel Adams, and John Hancock, the richest man in the province. Even Jonathan Sewell, a firm loyalist, was a regular visitor. Discussions centered on politics. John Adams was in his element, holding forth passionately with legal and philosophical opinions.

PROTESTING THE TOWNSHEND ACTS
Just as furor over the Stamp Act began to die down, Parliament and the king made another attempt to raise money from the reluctant colonies. This time, Charles Townshend, a member of Parliament, proposed a series of taxes on items that the colonists had to buy from Britain.

Among these were paint, paper, lead, and tea. Parliament quickly passed what came to be known as the Townshend Acts of 1767. Even worse, the king gave British tax collectors in the colonies the power to search homes, businesses, and ships. He wanted to make sure colonists were not smuggling goods into the colonies without paying taxes first.

John Hancock

❖

The colonists felt that Parliament and King George III were treating them as children who needed to be taught a lesson. Resentment and unrest simmered throughout the colonies. Once again, Boston became the center of political turmoil. That summer, British tax officials forced their way onto patriot John Hancock's boat, the *Liberty*. They took away goods that they claimed had been smuggled. When patriots protested, the British called Boston a "town ruled by mobs." The angry crowd attacked the tax collectors who were forced to flee for their lives.

John Adams composed a letter addressed to all colonists protesting the hated Townshend Acts. The Massachusetts legislature sent Adams's message to the other colonies, where it was read and discussed. The idealistic young lawyer also offered legal assistance to patriots who resisted the British. This help included defending his friend John Hancock against charges of smuggling.

Around this time, new songs of freedom began to be heard. One verse ran, "Then join hand in hand, brave Americans all, By uniting we stand, by dividing we fall." British customs commissioners responded with a tune called "Yankee Doodle." This song went, "Yankee Doodle came to town, a-riding on a pony, He stuck a feather in his hat and called it macaroni." It was meant to mock the colonists. Little did they know that one day this song would become a rallying cry for independence.

John Hancock's case was difficult for Adams. His opponent in court was another close friend, Jonathan Sewall, who was the crown (king's) prosecutor. The case dragged on all winter. Adams described it as "a painful Drudgery." Finally, his tireless defense forced the prosecution to withdraw the charges in March 1769.

At this point, John Adams found himself at a crossroads. Jonathan Sewall was moving to a new government position. He tried to convince Adams to become his replacement as crown prosecutor. If Adams accepted the job, he would be expected to win cases for the king against colonists. Still, it was a wonderful opportunity. It would ensure the ambitious young attorney a fine, prosperous career, a step up on "the ladder of royal favour and promotion."

John Adams saw the offer as a bribe to make him stop his patriot activities. He firmly refused. "I cannot in honor or conscience accept it," he wrote. Wealth and advancement were attractive, but John Adams would not compromise principles for personal advantage. Independence was essential to his existence.

THE BOSTON MASSACRE

While Adams had been defending John Hancock in court, the British had grown determined to put down unruly mobs that were protesting in the city. In the fall of 1768, warships arrived in Boston harbor and trained their guns upon the town. Four regiments of soldiers entered the city. When John Adams saw the red-coated troops marching down the streets, he wrote, "Their very Appearance in Boston was a strong proof to me, that the determination in Great Britain to subjugate [enslave] Us was too deep . . . ever to be altered by Us."

Adams had always been opposed to violence, but the actions of the British government convinced him that Britain would never treat the colonists fairly. Sending troops to occupy Boston had been the ultimate proof that the king was determined to control the colonists and treat them as enemies instead of British citizens. The soldiers showed contempt for the colonists. They jostled citizens off the sidewalks, striking them with the ends of their rifles. They beat small boys on the street and disturbed Sunday church services by firing guns and racing horses in the park. John Adams demanded an inquiry into the "Repeated offenses and Violences committed by the Soldiery against the people of Boston."

The presence of British troops in Boston enraged the public. Mobs set fire to the soldiers' quarters. Fights broke out regularly between the troops and the people. During one protest in 1770, a boy was killed. Two thousand angry, sorrowful Bostonians solemnly followed the child's funeral procession. "This Shewes [shows], there are many more Lives to spend if wanted in the Service of their Country,"

British soldiers shot point-blank into a crowd. The Boston Massacre worsened the tense relations between the British and the Bostonians.

John Adams noted. "The Ardor of the People is not to be quelled by the Slaughter of one Child."

A few days later, a belligerent crowd gathered on King Street in Boston. A foot of frozen March snow covered the ground. One British soldier was on guard. He sent for reinforcements, and seven more soldiers came running accompanied by their captain. The members of the mob jeered at and provoked the troops. They pelted the soldiers with snowballs, stones, and chunks of ice. The soldiers panicked and discharged their muskets. Five colonists were killed.

Word spread quickly about the "Boston Massacre." Public outrage rose to a boiling point. To everyone's surprise, John Adams agreed to defend the soldiers in court. It was his opinion that everyone was entitled to a fair trial. He believed that the colonies would suffer if angry mobs decided a person's guilt.

At the trial, Adams proved that the British captain was not guilty because he had not given an order to fire. The captain was set free, and only two of the soldiers received minor punishments. Again, Adams had been successful in court, but he was worried about his future. He thought that his political career would end. He expected the angry people of Boston to criticize him, and some did. Surprisingly, however, his popularity did not lessen. He was still accepted as a spokesman for the patriot cause. He spent endless, wearying hours attending meetings, discussing strategies, and writing opinions.

RETURN TO BRAINTREE

Soon after the trial, the Townshend Acts were repealed, except for the tax on tea. Tensions eased in Massachusetts and the other colonies. John Adams, exhausted from his work as a lawyer, selectman, and patriot, fell ill. Abigail had recently given birth to their second son, Charles. She, too, was weak and tired after bearing four children in six years. They decided their family would be better off in the healthy environment of the country.

A longing for his farm overtook Adams, and his thoughts began to center on "horses, oxen, cows, swine, walls, fences, etc." In the spring of 1771, he and Abigail moved their family back to the modest farmhouse in Braintree. Breathing the clean air of his native countryside restored John Adams's spirits. "Farewell politics," he wrote. "I . . . shall divide my time between law and husbandry [farming]."

This was not to be. Adams couldn't stay away from politics altogether. He kept his office in Boston and continued to attend meetings there with his cousin, Samuel Adams, and other patriots. As time went on, some Bostonians seemed to forget their treatment at the hands of the British. They were affectionate and respectful toward Massachusetts's new royal governor, Thomas Hutchinson, who had been appointed by the king. Not John Adams! He disapproved of Hutchinson. He blamed him for the "perpetual discontent and uneasiness between Britain and the colonies" and accused him of supporting an oppressive government. Adams believed that Britain would never stop trying to keep the colonies down. He predicted that eventually "a total opposition of interests shall take place" leading to war.

BACK TO BOSTON

Much as he loved the farm, John Adams was restless away from the center of controversy. After Abigail gave birth to a third son, Thomas Boylston, they decided to move back to Boston. In August 1772, they bought a brick house on Queen Street near Adams's office. Once there, he promised to stay away from "politics, political clubs, town meetings . . . etc." Of course, he did no such thing and was soon busy with political activities. As usual, he felt that he had failed to achieve anything worthwhile. "What an atom . . . I am," he complained to his diary. "My season for acquiring knowledge is past." John Adams was thirty-six years old.

Great Britain continued its campaign to weaken the colonies. Judges of the highest courts in the thirteen colonies had always been paid by the colonial legislature, which was elected by the colonists to make laws. Britain changed that policy. Judges were to receive their pay from the king. They would be more responsible to the king's wishes than to the rights of the citizens whose cases they judged. The new policy was one more way to take away colonial freedoms. In addition, Governor Hutchinson began to assert his power over that of the Massachusetts legislature. He claimed the right to overrule decisions of which he did not approve.

John Adams was disturbed by such bold attempts to lessen the ability of the colonies to govern themselves. He wrote a series of articles for the *Boston Gazette,* proving that the king and Parliament were trying to destroy the independence of colonial courts. His well-thought-out arguments brought more Americans over to the cause of freedom.

A few quiet months followed. The Adamses entertained friends. Several times they traveled back to the farm, where John Adams always found peace and contentment. They visited relatives and went to a wedding.

The peaceful times ended on December 17, 1773. Adams wrote in his diary, "Last night three cargoes of Bohea tea were emptied into the sea."

CHAPTER FIVE

ROAD TO REVOLUTION!

"Listen my children and you shall hear
Of the midnight ride of Paul Revere,
On the eighteenth of April, in Seventy-five...."
—from "Paul Revere's Ride,"
by Henry Wadsworth Longfellow

The electrifying event that Adams wrote about in his diary resulted from the hated Tea Act, passed by Parliament in May 1773. The Tea Act granted the British East India Company nearly exclusive rights to sell tea to the colonies. In addition to paying a tax, American merchants were being forced to buy their tea from just one company.

Protests arose in all the colonies. In Philadelphia and New York, the tea was refused and sent back to Britain. Merchants in Charleston, South Carolina, permitted the tea to be unloaded but did not offer it for sale. In Boston Governor Hutchinson ordered that the tea be unloaded. Crowds of angry Bostonians blocked the piers and would not let the tea be brought ashore. There were protests and meetings. The whole town became involved in the controversy. Some colonists began to arm themselves. If necessary, they would use force to keep the tea out of Boston. They planned to toll church bells if the tea were landed despite all their efforts. Abigail Adams wrote to a friend, "The Tea that bainfull weed is arrived. Great and I hope Effectual opposition has been made to the landing of it. . . . The flame is kindled and like Lightning it catches from Soul to Soul."

As 1773 came to a close, messages were sent to Governor Hutchinson asking him to support the people. On December 16, thousands of patriots gathered in and around the Old South Meeting House to await his reply.

Their hopes for a peaceful solution were crushed. The governor refused all their requests and once again ordered them to unload the tea. Samuel Adams spoke for all the townspeople when he declared, "This meeting can do nothing more to save the country." John Hancock supported him by asserting, "Let every man do what is right in his own eyes."

THE BOSTON TEA PARTY

The crowd marched to the docks. They were followed by war whoops and cries of "The Mohawks are come!" "Boston harbor a teapot tonight!" A group of rebels appeared. They were disguised as Mohawk Indians. They had blackened their faces, wrapped themselves in blankets, and brought axes and hatchets. Boarding the three ships, they hoisted the chests of tea onto the deck. Then they smashed them open with hatchets. The crowd watched in awed silence as the "Indians" tossed the tea into the water.

*In protest of British tea policies, Boston patriots hacked open
crates of tea and tossed them into Boston Harbor.*

◇

"What a cup of tea we're making for the fishes,"
remarked one man.

In less than three hours, 342 chests of tea were emptied
into Boston Harbor. Soon the Sons of Liberty were singing,
"Rally, Mohawks! Bring out your axes, and tell King George
we'll pay no taxes."

When John Adams received news of the "Boston Tea
Party," he wrote excitedly in his diary, "This is the most
magnificent Movement of all. . . . There is a Dignity, a

Majesty, a Sublimity, in this last Effort of the Patriots, that I greatly admire. . . . The People should never rise without doing something to be remembered."

Adams was more committed to the patriot cause than ever. No matter how far they had to go to obtain justice from Great Britain, he would stand with them. The American colonists had shown that they would not be forced into submission. However, Adams expressed a general fear when he worried about the future in his diary. What would the British government do in response to the colonists' rebellion?

The patriots waited uneasily for King George's next move. Preparing themselves for the worst, they secretly collected and stored gunpowder. Militia companies— armed groups of citizens—were formed and drilled. The patriots needed to be able to defend themselves against Britain if needed. During this stressful period, John Adams found some distraction by buying the house where he was born. "The Rocks and Trees, the . . . stream, the dark Thickett," he noted happily, "are all old Acquaintances of mine."

Five months after the Boston Tea Party, the British imposed a punishment upon the rebellious citizens in Massachusetts. Parliament passed four laws that became known as the Intolerable Acts. One of these laws ordered the port of Boston closed until the tea was paid for. Another law changed the nature of the Massachusetts legislature. Instead of the people electing legislators, the king's royal governor would appoint them. The governor was also given additional powers. These included the right to prohibit all town meetings. Thomas Gage,

General Thomas Gage

——————— ◇ ———————

who was commander of all British forces in the colonies, was appointed as the new governor. He had a reputation as a tough leader. There was no doubt that he would brutally enforce the new laws.

THE FIRST CONTINENTAL CONGRESS

Many of the colonists were enraged. They would not tamely accept such treatment. The legislature of Massachusetts called for a meeting of delegates, or representatives, from all the colonies to take place in Philadelphia. Members of the meeting would decide upon a united course of action. One of the five men chosen to speak for Massachusetts was John Adams. As usual, he questioned his abilities. "The Objects before me, are too grand . . . for my comprehension," he wrote. "We have not Men, fit for the Times."

The First Continental Congress began its meetings in Carpenters' Hall in Philadelphia on September 5, 1774. Many of the delegates were very conservative. They were reluctant to go against Britain. John Adams used all his powers of argument and reason to convince the delegates that they had to take a stand.

After seven weeks of discussion, the Congress voted to

Carpenters' Hall, the site of the First Continental Congress, was a large meeting space originally used by a carpenters' guild.

endorse a Declaration of Rights. This document would be circulated throughout the colonies and submitted to the king. It said that the Intolerable Acts were unlawful. Representatives called for a boycott on goods from Great Britain. They hoped the boycott would convince Parliament to repeal the Intolerable Acts. "This was one of the happiest days of my life," Adams wrote in his diary. "This day convinced me that America will support Massachusetts or perish with her." Congress's action proved to him that the rest of the colonies were willing to stand by Massachusetts, even if it meant risking punishment by Great Britain.

John Adams hated being away from Abigail and his

children for so long. He worried about them, especially when word came that British troops had shelled Boston and that Massachusetts militiamen were arming and building embattlements for defense. During the three months of their separation, Abigail had been forced to take charge of the business and financial end of the farm. This was in addition to her responsibilities for the house, the children, the garden, and the dairy. She somehow found time to write to her husband regularly. She kept him informed about details of day-to-day life on the farm as well as the events in Massachusetts.

In November John Adams was reunited with his family. He settled down to manage his businesses. Even more important, he wrote a series of articles. Adams's strengths were as a thinker and writer. He could make his greatest contributions to the patriot cause by using these skills. In the articles, known as the "Novanglus" essays, he argued that colonial legislatures, not Parliament, were supreme in America. He claimed that Parliament could regulate trade in America only with the consent of the colonies. Every week during the winter of 1774 and early 1775, he wrote articles for the *Boston Gazette,* backing up his ideas with historical and political facts. His articles helped spread ideas about rights and liberties throughout the colonies. He was admired for his thoughtful arguments on behalf of the colonies.

LEXINGTON AND CONCORD

On April 18, 1775, the antagonism between Britain and its American colonies came to a head. Just before midnight, General Gage ordered British troops to march to Concord, Massachusetts, for a secret attack. He commanded his

*When British troops arrived in Lexington, minutemen stood
ready to fire on them on the town's green.*

troops to seize the arms and powder that the colonists were
storing and to capture troublesome patriots like Sam Adams
and John Hancock. Patriot spies got word of Gage's order
and put into action a plan to stop him.

Two patriot riders named Paul Revere and William
Dawes galloped on horseback from Boston all through the
night alerting the countryside. Volunteer soldiers, known as
minutemen for their ability to be ready at a minute's
notice, jumped from their beds to prepare for battle. On
their way to Concord, the British troops reached the town
of Lexington. They found a group of Massachusetts minutemen waiting for them. Shots were fired, and eight
Americans fell dead. At Concord, too, patriots lined up to
resist. Here was fired "the shot heard round the world."

The American Revolution had begun.

CHAPTER SIX

THE BLOODY STRUGGLE FOR LIBERTY

"We hold these truths to be self-evident, that all men are created equal, that they are endowed by their Creator with certain unalienable Rights, that among these are Life, Liberty and the pursuit of Happiness."

—Thomas Jefferson,
the Declaration of Independence

The Battles of Lexington and Concord changed everything. They brought American colonies into open rebellion against Great Britain. Adams believed that the British had given them no choice but to submit or fight. "If We did not defend ourselves," John Adams wrote, "they would kill Us."

A Second Continental Congress met in Philadelphia on May 10, 1775. This time their task was more serious. They had to decide whether to give in to the king and Parliament or commit to a war for independence. Many

Americans still longed for reconciliation with Britain. They feared that the colonies would lose much more than they would gain if they went to war with Britain. Great Britain offered the colonies needed protection from traditional enemies, such as France and Spain. Just as important, Britain gave the colonies the stability of an established government. These delegates worried that the colonies could not survive without the monarchy.

Other delegates wanted a complete separation from Britain. Without it, they argued, freedom would never come. "Is life so dear or peace so sweet as to be purchased at the price of chains and slavery?" a patriot named Patrick Henry had asked in Virginia. "I know not what course others may take, but as for me, give me liberty or give me death."

Across the ocean in London, Parliament was also meeting. Some members, such as Edmund Burke and William Pitt, wanted to seek peace with their colonial cousins. But other members of Parliament overwhelmingly defeated them. Parliament voted to force the Americans to obey the king by any means necessary.

The debate raged longer in Philadelphia. John Adams was a passionate spokesman for independence. He saw clearly that the British government would never give the American colonies the freedoms they sought. Separation from Britain was their only choice.

Adams received letters from Abigail that described the panic spreading through Massachusetts as red-coated British soldiers ruthlessly tried to put down the rebellion. The news made Adams impatient with his long-winded colleagues. Abigail wrote about the fear she and other Massachusetts colonists were experiencing. "Does every

Member [of Congress] feel for us?" she asked. "Can they realize what we suffer?" Bitterly, her husband replied, "They cant, They dont. There are some persons in New York and Philadelphia to whom a ship is dearer than a City, and a few Barrells of flower [flour], than a thousand Lives."

While Congress debated and appointed committees to study the situation, the American Revolution, though still undeclared, was raging in Massachusetts. The American forces were ragged and unorganized. They needed a commander. John Adams gave much thought to this choice. Adams had become one of the leading figures in Congress, and he knew his opinions mattered. His recommendation would carry weight. His Boston friend, John Hancock, wanted the position badly. John Adams, however, was already thinking ahead to a union of thirteen squabbling colonies, each with different needs and beliefs.

Rebels from Massachusetts dominated the call for independence. Other colonies were less convinced of the need for war. Adams realized that a commander from the South would be in a better position to unite the factions. A Virginian with good qualifications happened to be available. On June 14, 1775,

✧ ————————————

George Washington had served with distinction in the British army during the French and Indian War.

John Adams stood before Congress to nominate a man with "Skill and Experience as an Officer, . . . independent fortune, great Talents, and excellent . . . Character." His name was George Washington, and he was immediately elected to be commander in chief of the Continental army.

Battles continued to rage in Massachusetts between the well-trained and well-equipped British troops and the volunteer soldiers who made up the colonial army. Abigail sent Adams letters detailing the bloody events. She wrote that she and their son John Quincy climbed to the top of a hill to watch the fighting unfold. They heard the thunder of British cannon during the Battle of Bunker Hill and watched the burning of nearby Charlestown. "Charlestown is laid in ashes," she wrote sadly.

Abigail and John Quincy watched the Battle of Bunker Hill from afar. A British bayonet charge was a decisive factor in the bloody battle, which the British won.

Abigail's letters to her husband took on new hope when General Washington arrived in Massachusetts to take command. "I was struck with General Washington," she wrote. She observed a gentleman of easy dignity. "Modesty marks every line and feature of his face."

PERSONAL LOSSES

The Continental Congress took a break during the summer of 1775, and Adams was able to return home. Tragic news awaited him. His brother Elihu had died from dysentery, an intestinal disease. John Adams wanted time to mourn his brother and be with his family, but duty called him away.

In September Congress met again, and he had to return to Philadelphia. Soon afterward, he learned from Abigail's letters that there was now an epidemic of dysentery in Braintree. To his horror, both Abigail and Tommy, who was three years old, became ill. Abigail's mother took care of them until they were well again. Then she caught the disease and died. For once, Abigail's letters displayed some weakness. "I am almost ready to faint under this severe and heavy stroke." She wrote sorrowfully about being separated from *thee,* who used to be a comforter to me in affliction."

DECLARING INDEPENDENCE!

In December 1775, Adams went home for a short visit but returned to Philadelphia a month later. By this time, there was more agreement in Congress about the need for independence. "We are in the very midst of a revolution," John Adams wrote. "The colonies must be declared free and independent states." A committee was appointed to draft a resolution. This statement would be the official announcement to the world that a

Benjamin Franklin, Adams, Philip Livingston of New York, and Roger Sherman of Connecticut made up the committee that helped Jefferson draft the Declaration of Independence.

new country had come into existence. It needed to be carefully worded in a way that would make the colonies' claim to independence clear and legitimate. Among the members of the new committee were John Adams, Thomas Jefferson from Virginia, and Benjamin Franklin from Pennsylvania. Thomas Jefferson agreed to write a draft of the statement, but he engaged in intense discussion with Adams, who suggested ideas and phrases to be included in the declaration.

The decision to declare independence from Britain was a momentous one. Many members of Congress were reluctant to break all ties. Some were fearful of opposing the greatest military power on earth. For Adams the answer was simple. "It is the will of Heaven," he wrote to Abigail, "that the two countries should be sundered [separated] forever."

For her part, Abigail thought long and hard about the kind of nation they were creating. She believed that slavery should be outlawed and that all black men, women, and children should be freed. She urged her husband to see to it that women received equal rights, including the right to vote. "Remember the Ladies," she told him. "[Women] will not hold ourselves bound by any Laws in which we have no voice." When her husband replied that "we [men] know better than to give up our...power," Abigail was furious. "Whilst you are proclaiming peace and good will to Men," she wrote back crossly, you keep "absolute power over Wives."

In addition to his work on the committee to draft a declaration of independence, Adams was also involved in war preparations. He had been newly appointed president of the Board of War, a committee dedicated to the management of the armed forces. He struggled constantly to obtain badly needed supplies, such as clothing, arms, ammunition, and food, despite a lack of funds. He worked day and night, while Congress endlessly debated separation from Britain.

On July 1, 1776, as a thunderous storm raged outside the hall, John Adams addressed the Congress. He had no notes for his speech but used the arguments he had laid out in earlier writings and speeches. Carefully and passionately, Adams outlined all his arguments in favor of independence.

Adams spoke for more than two hours. The power of his reasoning won over the delegates. The colonies voted overwhelmingly for independence. They resolved "that these United States are, and, of right ought to be, Free and Independent States, that they are absolved from all allegiance to the British crown, and that all political connexion

This painting by American artist John Trumbull depicts the signing of the Declaration of Independence. Adams is shown in the center of the room.

between them, and the state of Great Britain, is . . . totally dissolved."

Three days later on July 4, Congress approved a Declaration of Independence that had been written by Thomas Jefferson. Nearly all the delegates signed it, pledging their lives, their fortunes, and their honor to the cause of freedom. John Adams predicted that Congress's bold declaration would be marked by later generations each year, celebrated with "pomp and parades, with shows, games, sports, guns, bells, bonfires and illuminations from one end of this continent to the other."

In cities and villages throughout the colonies, people gathered to hear the news. Abigail Adams stood among an excited crowd near the State House in Boston where the declaration was read aloud. She wrote her husband how proud she was of his part in laying a foundation for the new nation.

The United States of America was born. For a long time, however, it looked as though the infant country would not survive. The odds were against the Americans. The men in the new American Continental army were untrained and poorly supplied. They fought bravely but were up against the most powerful army in the world. King George and Parliament sent their best generals and battle-proven troops to crush the rebellion. General Washington needed time to train his ragtag army.

In the meantime, the Americans lost almost every battle they fought. The worst defeat was in New York. The British believed that if they occupied New York and New Jersey, they could divide New England from the southern states and weaken the American alliance. The British general, Sir William Howe, gathered a large army in New York and forced George Washington's troops to retreat to New Jersey. The British followed relentlessly. They drove the Continentals through New Jersey to the Delaware River, as one bloody battle followed another.

THE SAD SEPARATION FROM ABIGAIL CONTINUES

In Philadelphia it seemed to John Adams that he had earned the right to go back to Massachusetts to be with his family. He had worked hard to create this struggling new nation. His nagging, lecturing, and brilliant arguments had convinced the other delegates to vote for independence. But his duties as president of the Board of War kept him in Philadelphia. He had to find supplies and arms for the army. The Continentals were in desperate need of more recruits, arms, food, and medicine. At forty years of age, John Adams was too old to fight in the Continental army, but he was determined to serve his country in every way possible.

Except for short visits home, Adams spent most of his

time apart from his wife and children. His devotion to the struggle for liberty demanded his complete attention. Abigail supported this decision. She understood that the cause in which they believed was greater than their personal needs. She encouraged him in the letters she wrote regularly and advised him about important issues.

Adams's separation from his family caused even more hardship when Abigail became pregnant again. She complained that even animals had a mate to sit with them. John was depressed that he could not be with Abigail. "Oh that I could be near," he wrote. During the summer of 1777, Abigail gave birth to a baby girl, who was born dead. Abigail and the other children wept. Three hundred miles away, the baby's father also mourned. He wondered whether future Americans would appreciate their sacrifices. "What have I suffered?" he wrote. "What have I not hazarded?"

In November of that year, John Adams finally went home. He had served in the Congress for almost four years and neglected his family and his business. While other lawyers in Massachusetts had been earning huge sums of money, Adams had given no time to his own law practice. His absence had "left my Accounts in very loose condition," he complained. "I was daily losing the fruits of seventeen Years industry . . . for no Man ever did so much Business for so little profit." Although the work he had done for his nation had earned him great respect, it left him with little money.

THE CALL TO FRANCE

John Adams told his wife that he was home to stay. But a few months later, duty called again. Congress asked him to join Benjamin Franklin in France and help convince the

French to aid the Americans with guns, money, and men. France was Britain's mortal enemy. They had been engaged in almost constant warfare for decades. France was a natural ally for Britain's rebellious colonies.

How could Adams refuse? The cause to which he had given his life was in grave danger. General Washington and his men were freezing and starving in Valley Forge, Pennsylvania, the Continental army's main camp. In February 1778, John Adams left for Paris. Abigail bravely kissed him good-bye. Adams took his oldest child, ten-year-old John Quincy, on the journey with him. Abigail gave strict instructions to the father. "Injoin it upon him," she said, "never to Disgrace his Mother, and to behave worthy of his Father." Abigail watched through a mist of tears as her husband and son set off on the long, dangerous journey across the sea.

——————————— ✧ ———————————

At the time Adams set out for France, Washington's troops were wintering at Valley Forge, where they faced cold weather, hunger, and sickness.

A Perilous Journey

Traveling across the ocean in 1778 could be dangerous. John Adams's trip to Paris was even more horrendous than the typical voyage of the time. Before his journey on the *Boston*, Adams's only experience with ocean travel had been short fishing trips in mild Massachusetts waters. An ocean voyage was something new for him. He asked hundreds of questions of the sailors and the captain, whose name was Samuel Tucker. Adams was temporarily quieted by a bout of seasickness but was soon up and about asking more questions and even making suggestions to the captain on better ways of handling the ship.

More exciting events soon occurred. Several times during the voyage, they encountered British ships. In one case, shots were exchanged, and the British captain surrendered his ship. It was sailed to Massachusetts by some of Captain Tucker's men, and the British crew were taken aboard the *Boston* as prisoners.

The next enemy they encountered was even deadlier than British guns. A torrential storm struck. It raged for three days, slamming the ship about like a toy boat. It was impossible to even stand up. People, tables, chests, and bottles were all tossed around. Twenty-three crewmen suffered injuries, and it seemed as though the ship would be wrecked. For John Adams, this experience was the thrill of a lifetime. He loved the danger and the challenge. He was later able to boast that "I was myself perfectly calm." The storm finally ended, but several others occurred during the voyage.

After six harrowing weeks at sea, the *Boston* finally put into the port of Bordeaux in France. John Adams's first trip across the Atlantic was at an end.

CHAPTER SEVEN

TRAVELS ABROAD

"The delights of France are innumerable. The politeness, the elegance . . . , the magnificence and splendor is beyond all description."
—John Adams

Adams was not pleased with the situation he found in Paris. The records of the American delegation in France were a mess. "There was never before I came," he complained, "a minute Book, a Letter Book or an Account Book." He set to work immediately trying to bring some order into the chaos.

Adams also disapproved of Benjamin Franklin's high style of living. Franklin was charming and sophisticated. He was often received at court in the palace by the king and queen, and he had become the darling of the French nobility. He looked for any opportunity to persuade influential people to help the American cause. Franklin moved in a whirl of parties, teas, and court dances. The lords and ladies of fashion snubbed plain-speaking John Adams. He

*While Adams worked at his desk, Benjamin Franklin endeared himself
to the members of the French royal court, especially the women.*

———————————————— ✧ ————————————————

spent his time at his desk sorting through piles of papers.
He conscientiously applied himself to the details that
Benjamin Franklin had neglected.

There was something else that irritated Adams even
more. It turned out that the important work had been
completed before his arrival. The French government had
already recognized the United States as an independent
nation. Treaties between the two nations had been signed.
These agreements stated that France would side with the
Americans in the war and provide them with funding.

Adams was annoyed at this waste of his time and effort.
He advised Congress that one minister to France would be

enough and suggested that expense accounts be strictly controlled. This was an obvious criticism of Franklin's costly spending habits. Months passed. Adams did his best to put affairs in order. He also sent John Quincy to a boarding school at Passy near Paris. Here the boy tried to follow the advice his mother had given him to "improve your understanding for acquiring usefull knowledge and virtue."

Adams longed for his wife. Abigail, too, was unhappy. "How lonely are my days? How solitary are my nights?" she wrote him in December 1778. That winter was harsh. Money was tight in Braintree. The costs of food soared due to the war. Abigail had to scrimp and make do with what she had.

ADAMS FAMILY REUNITES

In February 1779, Adams learned that Congress had finally taken his advice to reduce the members of the American delegation in Paris. They appointed Franklin the sole minister to France. Later that spring, more than a year after Adams had left Massachusetts, he and his son set sail aboard the *Sensible,* bound for Boston.

The family was happily reunited. Adams got acquainted again with his other children. He even found time to produce, almost single-handedly, a new constitution for the state of Massachusetts. The constitution would set down the rights of the state's people and a new system of government.

Adams modeled his state's constitution on his own earlier writings, the Declaration of Independence, and other newly adopted state constitutions. He based the constitution on the central idea that all men are born free and independent and are entitled to inalienable, or guaranteed, rights. These rights included the right to happiness, the right to defend one's life and freedoms, and the right to own and protect property. Adams also added a guarantee of free elections. Other freedoms included the freedoms of speech and press and the right of trial by jury.

Adams also spent time considering the best government for his state. In the Massachusetts constitution, he divided the government into legislative (congress), executive (governor), and judicial (courts and judges) branches. Each branch would have a say in how to run the state. That way, no one part of the government could become too powerful. He completed his draft of the constitution in October, and it was eventually adopted in March 1780.

NEW DUTIES ABROAD

Shortly after John Adams finished his draft of the Massachusetts constitution, Congress asked him to return to France to begin work on a peace treaty between the United States of America and Great Britain. The tide of war had turned. The Continentals were now winning battles. British troops were retreating. Congress believed that the war would soon end. They needed someone clever and efficient to negotiate this treaty.

In November 1779, John Adams sailed for Europe once again with John Quincy, now twelve. This time he also took along nine-year-old Charles. Their destination was France, where the treaty negotiations would take place. Abigail was left behind with fourteen-year-old Nabby and young Thomas, who was seven. Before leaving, Adams pressed a note into his wife's hand. "We shall yet be happy," he wrote. It is certain that Abigail wanted to believe that. She was saddened and depressed to have their family broken up again. Once again, however, her dedication to the cause gave her the courage and strength to accept another separation.

Adams put both boys into school in Paris. Then he faced up to the problem of working with Benjamin Franklin again. These two had managed to work together in Philadelphia to unite the colonies and declare independence. In France they were like oil and water. Adams felt that Franklin was so busy impressing the French with his charm that he was not looking out for the best interests of America. Franklin found Adams too conscientious and judgmental. He thought that Adams rubbed people the wrong way. Benjamin Franklin's gift was to be liked by all. He easily made friends who were important to the future of the new nation. Adams's brilliance was to craft a treaty that would help the United States.

John Adams was not tactful. He spoke his mind straight and to the point. That made him some enemies. One diplomat described him as "the most ungracious man I ever saw." Franklin complained about him to Congress.

Adams was in a fury over Franklin's complaints. He did not understand or respect the French diplomats who were helping to negotiate a peace treaty between the British and the Americans. The French wanted clauses in the treaty that were not in the best interests of America. Adams stubbornly refused. This led to quarrels with the French ministers. Adams realized his presence in Paris was troublesome. Eager to get away, he took the boys on a trip to Amsterdam, the capital of the Netherlands. Adams hoped he would be able to persuade the Dutch government to recognize the United States as an independent country.

*Amsterdam sits at the junction of two rivers and is crossed by canals.
During the 1700s, the city was an important center for banking.*

─────────────── ✧ ───────────────

In Amsterdam Adams put the boys in Latin school and
began to try getting support from the Dutch. Congress recognized his value there and appointed him temporary minister to the Netherlands. His task was to obtain a treaty of
friendship and commerce with the Dutch. Adams met with
Dutch statesmen and bankers. They were fearful of antago-
nizing the British, but the new American minister wrote a
persuasive paper. It listed the historical ties between
America and the Netherlands. Adams made convincing
arguments that a treaty with America would also be to their
advantage.

In July 1781, Adams's secretary, Francis Dana, was
appointed minister to Russia. Dana did not know any
Russian. He did not even speak French, which was the

John Quincy Adams in his teens
——————— ◇ ———————

language of diplomats everywhere. John Quincy, now fourteen, was proficient in French. His father remarked that the boy wrote better in French than in English. Adams permitted his son to travel with Dana to Russia to be his interpreter. John Quincy remained there for more than a year. Eleven-year-old Charles was miserable in the Netherlands without the company of his brother. He felt ill and begged to go home. His father wrote to Abigail that it would break the boy's heart to keep him there any longer. He put Charles aboard a ship for the return voyage home.

Then the glorious news arrived that on October 19, 1781, British general Cornwallis had surrendered his army to General Washington. John Adams regretted being so far away from his native land in its hour of victory, but he had an important job to do. He succeeded brilliantly in the Netherlands. The Dutch recognized the independence of the United States. In July 1782, they signed a treaty of friendship and trade between the nations. Adams also obtained loans totaling $3.5 million dollars. These funds would help the young nation keep going until a newly formed government took over.

*The British surrendered to Washington after they lost a
key battle in Yorktown, Virginia.*

WORKING ON A PEACE TREATY

After obtaining recognition from the Netherlands, John
Adams returned to Paris. The British and Americans had
agreed to negotiate a peace treaty in the French capital
because it was a neutral setting with ties to both countries.
Congress appointed Benjamin Franklin and John Jay, a delegate from New York, to work with Adams on the U.S.
peace commission. It was the job of the commission to
negotiate details of the treaty with Great Britain. They
talked and argued with the British representatives. Adams
was often angered by the stubbornness of the British commissioners. But he and the other men worked hard to come
up with a treaty both countries could sign.

The negotiations continued into 1783. Finally, on September 3, the Treaty of Paris was signed. It officially ended the Revolutionary War. Adams was pleased with the work he had done. He had successfully set boundaries between Canada and the United States. This established America's rights to all the land up to the Canadian border. Adams also had insisted on securing U.S. fishing rights in the Atlantic Ocean, even in the waters off British territory in Canada and Newfoundland. The ability to fish in these waters was of vital importance to fishers all along the eastern coast.

John Adams had achieved another success for the nation he loved, but he still could not go home. Congress asked him to remain in France to arrange a commercial treaty with Britain, allowing for trade between the two nations. These treaties would enable the new country to trade with businesses abroad and build a strong American economy. The thought of another winter away from Abigail was unbearable. Abigail, too, had complained, at times bitterly, about the long separation from her husband. He asked her to join him in Europe. "I am so unhappy without you," he wrote.

ABIGAIL COMES TO PARIS

In the spring of 1784, Abigail Adams put her two youngest children in the care of relatives. On June 20, accompanied by her daughter, Nabby, she set sail to reunite with her husband. They had been apart for nearly five years.

Abigail and Nabby were deathly ill with seasickness during a dreadful four-week voyage. They arrived in Britain in July 1784. John Adams joined them in August and took them to Paris. There, Abigail was astounded and amused by French fashions and pleasures. "The fashionable shape of

*In Paris Abigail discovered she enjoyed entertainment
such as ballets and operas.*

the ladies here," she wrote to a friend, "is to be very small
at the bottom of the waist, and very large round the shoul-
ders." She enjoyed the ballet, though some of the perfor-
mances shocked her. "The dresses and beauty of the
performers were enchanting," she said in a letter, "but no
sooner did the dance commence than I was ashamed to . . .
look at them . . . spring two feet from the floor . . . showing
their garters and drawers."

While Abigail and her daughter enjoyed the sights of
Paris, her husband remained hard at work on his country's
business. By this time, Thomas Jefferson had replaced
Franklin as minister to France. Since meeting each other at

Thomas Jefferson

———— ✦ ————

the Continental Congress, Adams and Jefferson had kept up a friendship through letters. In France the two men got along extremely well and spent many pleasurable hours together.

John Adams and Thomas Jefferson were an odd couple. They were different in many ways. John Adams was a New Englander from a modest, hardworking farming background. Jefferson was a southern aristocrat from a family of wealthy landowners. Adams was outgoing, hot-tempered, talkative, and opinionated. Jefferson was reserved, quiet, cool, and intellectual. They had in common, however, two important things. Both were passionate about knowledge and learning. They were also equally committed to the concepts of justice and freedom that had brought about the American Revolution and American independence. Abigail, too, was fond of Jefferson. She called him "one of the choice ones of the earth."

AMBASSADOR TO BRITAIN

On February 13, 1785, John Adams was appointed the first American ambassador to Britain. He had been hoping for months to get this position as a reward for his diplomatic successes. Some delegates in Congress who did not like Adams spoke up against him. It hurt him that these men opposed him so strongly after all he had given for his country. Nevertheless, Congress approved his appointment by a large majority.

Adams and Abigail decided to send John Quincy home to attend Harvard. In May Adams, Abigail, and Nabby left Paris for Britain.

By this time, Adams's appreciation of France had grown, and he was sad to leave. When someone remarked that he was going to his family's ancestral homeland in Britain, he replied, "I have not one drop of blood in my veins, but what is American." He especially regretted having to say good-bye to his good friend Thomas Jefferson. After Adams left, Jefferson wrote to him. "The departure of your family has left me in the dumps."

John and Abigail Adams would miss the kindness of the friends they had made in France. They wondered how they would be treated by the British, who had so recently been their bitter enemies.

CHAPTER EIGHT

AMBASSADOR ADAMS

"An Ambassador from America!
Good heavens what a sound!"
—comment in a London newspaper
on the arrival of John Adams

John and Abigail Adams had good reason to worry about their reception in the British capital. Many British citizens were furious that their country had been forced to sign a peace treaty with those boorish, ungrateful colonists who had dared to create a nation of their own. Fortunately, the new ambassador received a warm official welcome from the British foreign secretary, Lord Carmarthen. Adams was told that the king himself would meet with him in a few days.

The lawyer from Massachusetts was nervous about the audience with King George. He was the ruler who had oppressed the colonists. He had sent heavily armed forces to break their will and destroy them. How would he treat someone who was now the representative of an independent nation, the United States of America?

John Adams spent the next days learning the rituals of court procedure and composing a short speech. The meeting went better than he expected. He conveyed to the king the wishes of the American people for his health and happiness and spoke feelingly about "restoring . . . esteem, confidence, and affection . . . between people who . . . have the same language . . . and kindred blood." King George responded graciously, and an amiable conversation followed. The king even expressed a wish for Great Britain to form a friendship with the United States as an independent nation.

Adams was relieved. He now believed his time in London would be "less painful than I once expected." He realized, however, that a pleasant meeting with the king did not mean his mission in Britain would be successful. Adams recognized that a smile from the king meant little. The ambassador's dealings would be with the smooth but hard-nosed politicians who carried out the actual tasks of the king's government. Most of his meetings were with Lord Carmarthen.

THE TREATY OF PARIS

One of Adams's main tasks was to straighten out points in the Treaty of Paris over which Great Britain and the United States still disagreed. The British had not removed all their troops from American soil as stated in the treaty. Adams discovered that they had no intention of doing so until Americans paid their debts to creditors in Britain.

Adams also hoped to convince Britain to reopen British ports to American ships. America's economy was in a bad state after the years of war. The country desperately needed opportunities to buy British goods and sell their own. Not only were American ships kept out of ports in Britain, but the British also excluded them from Canada and the British West Indies. Adams hoped to solve these and other differences. The British officials, such as Lord Carmarthen, kept placing blocks in his path.

The U.S. government was a young, struggling nation. Since 1781 it had been governed by the Articles of Confederation, a set of agreements that bound the thirteen states together. But the confederation had very little power. It did not allow for the collecting of countrywide taxes or the enforcing of national laws. Individual states still had great independence and did not always agree on how to best run the country. There was a great deal of squabbling and confusion.

The British took advantage of the weakness of the United States by refusing to agree to any of Adams's requests on behalf of his country. They hoped that the new nation would fall apart before it had fully begun. It would be a sweet revenge for them to be able to regain their former colonies. For the rest of his mission in Britain, Adams would have countless meetings with British representatives. They all ended in failure. "We hold conference after conference," he complained in a letter to Thomas Jefferson, "but the ministers . . . have no plans."

LIFE IN BRITAIN WITH
AMBASSADOR ADAMS AND FAMILY

Personally, John Adams was happier than he had been in a long time. Abigail and Nabby were with him. They moved into a large townhouse in Grosvenor Square in the heart of London. Abigail thought it was "one of the finest squares in London. The air is as pure as it can be."

Adams and Abigail entertained many new British friends, as well as travelers from America and other countries. They were on a tight budget, and Abigail did the shopping and cooking herself, unusual duties for an ambassador's wife. They were invited to elegant parties and receptions. Despite these good times, Abigail was not completely happy in Britain. She disliked the way many British people treated Americans, and she sorely missed her children. Adams also missed his farm in Braintree and often thought of it when strolling through the farms and countryside of Britain.

Nabby had a wonderful time in the social whirl of London. Even more exciting, she fell in love. Colonel William Stephens Smith had served honorably with

─────── ✦

In London Nabby Adams met other Americans, including the artist Mather Brown, who painted this portrait of her.

, General Washington. He later became Adams's secretary in London. William and Nabby spent much time together. In June 1786, they were married in the house on Grosvenor Square. A year later, John Adams's first grandson, William Steuben Smith, was born in London. Both Adams and Abigail were thrilled.

Meanwhile, Adams continued to experience only frustration on the diplomatic front. His conferences with Lord Carmarthen were fruitless. All the American ambassador's proposals were met with icy indifference or long delays. Letters flew back and forth between Adams and Thomas Jefferson, who was having similar problems in France.

John Adams was eager to accomplish something worthwhile for his new country. He busied himself with a new writing project. The book that resulted was published in early 1787. It was titled *A Defence of the Constitutions of Government of the United States of America.* Here Adams outlined his ideas for a permanent government in the United States.

Adams was frustrated with his lack of progress in Britain. He wrote to Congress asking to be relieved of his position as ambassador. By this time, a Constitutional Convention had convened in Philadelphia. Congress was trying to establish a body of laws for the new nation. John Adams's expertise was badly needed for this crucial project. His work in Europe was just as important, however, and Congress insisted that he remain there.

Although Adams could not attend the Constitutional Convention, his ideas about a new government influenced members of the meeting. Adams had the knowledge and understanding necessary to write a constitution. The framers of the U.S. Constitution knew this. They used

While Adams worked in London, members of Congress, including George Washington and Benjamin Franklin, signed the U.S. Constitution.

---

many concepts from his books and articles. They also followed the example that he had set in the constitution of Massachusetts. John Adams was not present when the U.S. Constitution was being written, but his imprint was firmly stamped upon it.

HOME AT LAST!

Adams finally received instructions from Congress to return to the United States. In the spring of 1788, he and Abigail left Britain. In June they sailed into Boston Harbor. A cheering crowd of thousands of people lined the docks to greet them. Cannons roared and church bells rang out in their honor. John Hancock, who had become governor of Massachusetts, escorted them to his mansion.

Adams and Abigail were speechless. They had never dreamed of receiving such a welcome. It warmed their hearts to see how well their nation understood and appreciated their dedication and sacrifices to the cause of freedom.

CHAPTER NINE

VICE PRESIDENT ADAMS

"Is not my election to this office . . .
a curse rather than a blessing?"
—John Adams commenting on
the office of vice president

John Adams had been abroad for nine years. He wondered what sort of country he was returning to. Much had changed since he had left for Europe. The country was no longer at war, but it was a land that had been ravaged. The new nation struggled with a lack of money. Unemployment and growing divisions among the states also weakened the country. America desperately needed unity and a stable government.

A step in the right direction took place in February 1789, when the first presidential election was held. The new Constitution established an Electoral College to choose the president and vice president. These electors were chosen by the states. Each elector cast two votes. The candidate who received the majority of votes would be president. The candidate with the next highest number would become vice president. Few doubted who the first president would be. No man in the country was as respected, admired, and loved as George Washington. He alone had the prestige and acceptance to glue together a union that was already showing signs of coming apart.

Politics and government were far from their thoughts when the Adamses returned from Europe. Family concerns were their first priority. They had purchased a new house in Braintree. It was damaged and filled with dust and needed a lot of repair. Months of hard work lay ahead. Adams and Abigail didn't mind. For the first time in many years, they were reunited with all three of their boys. John Quincy had completed law school and was working in Boston. Charles and Thomas were at Harvard. Only Nabby was missing from the family home. She was living in New York with her husband and child.

Adams worked on his house and spent time with his family. He unpacked his books and strolled about the farm with old friends. In a letter to Thomas Jefferson, he described what a luxury it was to be a private citizen. But Adams had served his country too long to turn from it for more than a short time. He was one of the founders of the United States and one of the few leaders who had a clear grasp of the issues. It was natural for him to be nominated as a presidential candidate in 1789, together with George Washington and several others. The result for president was unanimous. Every elector cast a ballot for George Washington. Each elector had two ballots, and Adams won more of these additional votes than any other nominee.

Therefore, George Washington won the presidential election, with Adams coming in second.

The United States of America had its first administration—President George Washington of Virginia and Vice President John Adams of Massachusetts. Adams was fifty-four years old.

VICE PRESIDENT ADAMS

The capital of the new nation was in New York. Adams went alone, but he couldn't bear being without Abigail again. Although they had little money to spare for the journey, he begged her to come. He instructed her to sell anything necessary to raise funds. Abigail hurried to be at the side of her husband, where exciting political decisions were being made. She was also eager to be near Nabby. Abigail and Adams moved into a house on Staten Island.

The new government had a lot of work ahead. There

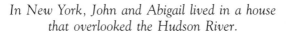

*In New York, John and Abigail lived in a house
that overlooked the Hudson River.*

were no traditions or past rules to guide the first administration and legislature. The leaders of the United States had to create policies through trial and error. John Adams, as usual, had no shortage of opinions on how everything in the new government should be conducted. These ranged from how the president should be addressed to the specific duties of the vice president.

The Constitution had limited the role of the vice president. The main purpose of the office was to have someone ready to be president in case the current president died. The vice president also presided over the meetings of the Senate, the upper house of the U.S. Congress. The position did not appeal much to a man who was accustomed to taking strong actions. John Adams described the vice presidency as "the most insignificant office that ever the invention of man contrived."

John Adams had no intention of being quiet and insignificant. He made the most of his role as president of the Senate. He spoke to the members at length, instructing and advising them on every issue that came up. They grew impatient with his long-winded speeches and ridiculed him. They called him "His Rotundity," referring to his short, fat figure.

The senators were even more annoyed when Adams lectured them about the office of the president. He thought that people would respect the president more if he appeared in "dignity and splendor." He even favored calling the president "His Highness the President." The legislators grew sick of these orations. They ruled that only senators would be permitted to debate in the Senate. The sole function of the vice president was to cast a deciding ballot in case of a tie. Ties happened often during the early years of the country. Adams was able to cast a deciding ballot on many important measures. Usually, he supported George Washington's policies.

His duties as vice president took up only a small part of the day. Adams spent his free time working on a series of newspaper essays that were eventually printed as a book. He called the essays "Discourses on Davila." In them he discussed his fears of permitting the common people to have too much power over the nation. He was thinking of a bloody revolution like the one that had begun in France. Like the American Revolution, the rebellion in France was based on the ideals of liberty and citizens' rights. However, the French Revolution had not led to democracy and peace. Bloodshed continued among various groups, and French citizens were terrorized by the rebels.

The French government seemed powerless in the face of a violent rebellion. John Adams didn't want something similar to happen to the United States. He called for a strong federal government to unify and stabilize the country as a whole. He also emphasized a need for balance of powers among the branches of government so that no one part of the government could gain complete control of the nation. His enemies distorted his words. They accused him of being a monarchist, someone who favors rule by a king.

POLITICAL PARTIES BEGIN TO TAKE SHAPE

John Adams was not a monarchist. As time went on, however, he came to believe more and more in a strong central government as a way of unifying the country. This brought him into conflict with his longtime friend Thomas Jefferson.

Jefferson trusted the goodness and wisdom of the people to make sound decisions for the government. He opposed too much central authority because he thought it might lessen individual freedoms. This difference, among others, brought about the formation of political parties. Alexander Hamilton, the secretary of the treasury, led the Federalists. They favored a strong national government, along with a centralized financial system and a powerful national army and navy. Thomas Jefferson's party wanted more power for states and individual citizens. His party was called the Anti-Federalists or Republicans. Later, it became known as the Democratic-Republican Party.

Alexander Hamilton

──────── ✧ ────────

In 1792 a second presidential election took place. Washington was expected to remain president. But Adams faced opposition in his bid to remain as vice president. His enemies accused him of being undemocratic. This criticism hurt him deeply. Adams had devoted his life to the cause of freedom and felt unappreciated. Adams and Abigail went to Braintree to escape the nastiness of the election. When the results were in, George Washington was reelected president, and John Adams once more was chosen as vice president.

Adams returned to his duties in Philadelphia, where the

capital had been moved. His role in the government seemed less and less important. "I have scarcely the power to do good or evil," he complained.

THE ELECTION OF 1796

Four years later, George Washington announced that he would not accept a third four-year term as president. Everyone believed that he wanted John Adams to take his place. "I am heir apparent, you know," he told Abigail. "A succession is soon to take place." Most people took their cue from George Washington and assumed that John Adams was the logical choice. Adams himself looked forward to a position where his vast experience, knowledge, and understanding of government would be used for the benefit of his country. He also believed that he deserved this honor.

The election of 1796 set the pattern for future U.S. elections. There were rival candidates and parties. The choice narrowed down to one between John Adams and Thomas Jefferson. The two candidates remained in the background. Their supporters, however, fought hard. Both sides hurled nasty accusations at the other candidate. The result was a close election. Adams was elected president, followed closely in votes by Jefferson. This would be the only time that the U.S. president and vice president came from different political parties.

John Adams was inaugurated president in Philadelphia on March 4, 1797. He described it as "a solemn scene . . . made more affecting to me by the presence of the General [George Washington]." Adams also reported that Washington told him, "Ay! I am fairly out and you fairly in. See which of us will be the happiest."

CHAPTER TEN

PRESIDENT ADAMS

*"It is universally admitted that Mr. Adams is a
man of incorruptible integrity."*
—Benjamin Franklin Bache, American journalist
and grandson of Benjamin Franklin

"President by three votes!" The small number of electoral
votes by which John Adams was elected over Jefferson
showed the divisions that had arisen in the United States.
The Federalist and Anti-Federalist Parties were growing further and further apart. The nation's respect for George
Washington had made it possible for him to keep the
squabbling factions under control. Once he was out of
office, the splits became deeper and more open. Eager,
ambitious men competed for power in the government.
They sometimes put their own interests over what was best
for the country.

John Adams was elected with the support of the
Federalist Party. It was no secret that Alexander Hamilton

was the true leader of the Federalists. His policies and orders, not those of the president, were followed by Federalists in the government. Even members of the president's cabinet, his closest advisers, were under Hamilton's influence. The new president agreed with the Federalist concept of a strong central government, but he was too independent minded to follow every wish of his party. This brought him into conflict with Hamilton, who was trying to control every aspect of government. Once Adams recognized Hamilton's influence, he told his cabinet clearly that they must accept his own power and decisions as president.

On the other side, Adams faced the demands of the Anti-Federalists, led by Vice President Thomas Jefferson. Adams struggled constantly to keep some sort of balance between these opposing forces and was usually successful. The constant need to do this, however, took its toll on John Adams. He was often tired and irritable. He worked hard but recognized that there was only so much he could do. "My administration will certainly not be easy to myself," he wrote. "It will be happy, however, if it is honorable."

THE THREAT FROM FRANCE

The most immediate problem was the threat of war with France. A long conflict had been going on between France and Great Britain. The United States had tried to remain neutral. Several years earlier, however, the United States had signed a treaty, known as the Jay Treaty, with Britain. This treaty had angered the French. They began attacking American shipping, and they sent the U.S. ambassador home.

By the time Adams took office, America's two political parties had formed strong opinions about how to deal with France. Alexander Hamilton used his influence to agitate for an immediate declaration of war against France. Thomas Jefferson and his followers urged America to support its former ally. The president wanted to avoid war altogether. In addition to all its usual horrors, any war would be bad for the country at this time because of its economic and military weaknesses. George Washington had advised the United States against foreign entanglements. Adams believed this was a wise policy to follow.

Adams called a special session of Congress to argue for neutrality and peace. In front of the lawmakers, he criticized the actions of France, while upholding the importance of friendly relations with the European nation. A few days later, he appointed a commission to negotiate a peaceful settlement with France.

Months passed with no results. Adams still wanted to maintain peace, but he believed that the United States had to negotiate from a position of strength. He urged Congress to increase America's military defenses in case of a French attack.

Reports began to trickle home from the American representatives in France that French agents had asked the United States for a bribe. Unless the United States paid French agents $250,000, they would not proceed with peace negotiations. The agents also expected the United States to lend France $10 million.

These reports did not mention the French agents by name but called them X, Y, and Z. This XYZ affair, as it was called, aroused much anti-French feeling in the United

This political cartoon from the time of the XYZ affair shows American representatives resisting the demands of a greedy French monster.

States. Alexander Hamilton took advantage of the public mood to influence Congress to break all treaties with France. Congress also expanded the army and created a new Department of the Navy. War seemed so close that George Washington was called out of retirement to lead the army.

Adams supported this strong stand, but he still hoped to avoid war. He considered sending a new mission to France to restart negotiations. But his cabinet, under the secret urgings of Alexander Hamilton, advised against this move.

Adams had a difficult decision to make. If he went against the wishes of his cabinet, he risked losing the support of the Federalists. But if he gave up on negotiations with France, his country might be forced to enter a costly war. The president's own son helped him with this important choice. Thomas Adams returned from a trip to Europe with a letter from the foreign minister of France. The message requested the president to send another delegate to

France. The French minister promised that the American representative would be received with the respect "suitable to the envoy of a free, independent and powerful nation."

John Adams had never been afraid to take a firm stand when he thought it was right. He ignored the advice of his cabinet. He did not even consult Congress. On his own, he appointed a new delegation to travel to France and negotiate a treaty.

THE ALIEN AND SEDITION ACTS

While President Adams was doing his best to avoid conflict with France, the nation was in the grip of war hysteria. In the face of a possible war with France, some members of the public feared the negative effects of political attacks on Adams and the Federalists. They worried that spies and traitors within the United States might be aiding the enemy by weakening the government. One method they might use would be to turn the public against the government with critical newspaper and magazine articles.

The Federalists in Congress used this mood as an excuse to pass the Alien and Sedition Acts. These laws made it illegal for anyone to speak or publish criticism of government officials. Anti-Federalists and others who disagreed with the government's policies were no longer able to speak freely.

John Adams did not propose these acts, but he signed them. He felt the extreme measures were necessary for national defense. These Alien and Sedition Acts were an attack upon a free press. Several newspaper publishers were arrested and convicted for writing articles opposing government policy. Anti-Federalists called this a "Federalist reign of terror." James Madison said that it was "a monster that

The peace treaty between France and the United States that Adams arranged was signed at the Convention of Mortefontaine in France.

———————————— ✧ ————————————

must forever disgrace its parents." The Alien and Sedition Acts expired in 1801.

In the meantime, negotiations with France continued. Adams wanted France to believe that the United States was ready and willing to defend itself if necessary. But he deeply hoped war could be avoided. Popular opinion, however, was on the side of those who urged war. John Adams's popularity would have soared if he had gone to war with France. He knew he was risking his career by opposing the conflict.

He struggled long and hard with each decision during this crisis. As always, John Adams's integrity and devotion to his country won out over personal needs. He placed the welfare of the United States and its people above his own political interests. He knew that a war with France would be harmful to the United States and did everything in his power to avoid it. In 1800, just before the end of Adams's presidency, a peace agreement was reached between France and the United States. The threat of war was over.

THE ELECTION OF 1800

John Adams's patience and wisdom had paid off for his country but not for himself. News of the peace agreement was not received until after the election of 1800. Meanwhile, Adams's enemies had been working against his reelection. Thomas Jefferson's supporters hurled slanderous, untrue accusations at the president. They accused him of being a monarchist, a fool, an evil old man. They even charged that he was insane. Adams's supporters were just as nasty in smearing Thomas Jefferson. They called him godless, cowardly, and immoral. Adams was put at a disadvantage when his former Federalist friends campaigned against him, urged on by Alexander Hamilton. Their candidate, a politician and general from South Carolina named Charles Cotesworth Pinckney, was defeated, but so was Adams. Thomas Jefferson won the election.

John Adams was stunned. He felt that the people and country he had served so long had rejected him. Even his own party had turned against him. Sadly, he went about completing the business of his administration. One of his last acts as president was to appoint forty-three judges who would continue to support a Federalist viewpoint even during a Jefferson administration. Among these judges was John Marshall, who became an influential and historic chief justice of the U.S. Supreme Court, the leading judge of the nation's highest court.

Just a few months earlier, the nation's capital had been moved permanently to the District of Columbia. The Adamses were the first family to occupy the building that became known as the White House. It was enormous and impressive, but it was still unfinished. The mansion looked like a castle in a muddy swamp.

"Not one room or chamber is finished," Abigail wrote. She complained about the large number of fires that had to

In 1800, when the White House was first occupied, Washington, D.C.,
was swampy and sparsely populated.

———————————— ✧ ————————————

be kept going to avoid sleeping in "wet & damp places."
She did her best, however, to add some elegant furnishings
and make it a home fit for the president of the United
States. "I pray heaven to bestow the best of blessings on
this house and all that shall hereafter inhabit it," John
Adams wrote. "May none but wise and honest men ever
rule under this roof!"

John and Abigail Adams only occupied the White
House for a few months. Abigail left first to go home to
Quincy (formerly called Braintree) and prepare for her hus-
band's return. Adams stayed in Washington to pack his
books and papers. In the early hours of the morning on
March 4, 1801, John Adams quietly left the capital.

It was the day of Thomas Jefferson's inauguration. The
outgoing president was too hurt to attend.

THOMAS JEFFERSON, FRIEND AND FOE

The great friendship between Jefferson and Adams had its share of ups and downs. Their relationship grew closest during the time they both lived in France. But it began to cool after both were back on American soil and after the men became involved in the turmoils of government and politics. They found themselves on opposite sides on many issues. The rift widened when Jefferson wrote a preface to a book by the patriot writer Thomas Paine. In it Jefferson seemed to criticize Adams for some of his Federalist ideas.

Adams was hurt and furious. Jefferson tried to apologize saying that "nothing was further from my intention . . . than to have had either my own or your name brought before the public." Adams angrily refused to accept this explanation. The breaking point was reached during the presidential election of 1800. The personal attacks that Jefferson's supporters made against Adams were too much to bear. When Adams lost that election, he and Jefferson no longer communicated.

In 1812, with both men retired, they finally resumed their correspondence. "A letter from you," Jefferson wrote, "calls up recollections very dear to my mind." They rediscovered the pleasure of exchanging letters and continued to do so until the last years of their lives.

John Adams and Thomas Jefferson died on the same day, July 4, 1826, the fiftieth anniversary of the Declaration of Independence. As Adams lay dying, his last words were "Jefferson still survives." Actually, Jefferson had passed away just a few hours earlier.

CHAPTER ELEVEN

THE FINAL YEARS

"He died in good old age,
full of days . . . and honor."
—Pastor Peter Whitney
of Quincy, Massachusetts, on John Adams

When John Adams left the presidency in 1801, he was sixty-five years old. He would never again be active in public life. His term as president had been filled with problems and controversy. He felt he had been slandered by his enemies and rejected by the American people. An ungrateful country seemed to have forgotten how much he had sacrificed to create it.

To make matters worse, he was burdened with family problems. Abigail was not well. She had been sick on and off with unknown fevers and ailments that left her weak and frail. Their children were having problems too. Charles suffered from alcoholism. For years his frantic family had watched as he slowly drank himself to death. Charles's tragic life ended when he was only thirty years old. Nabby was also in trouble. Her husband was unreliable and often left his family for months at a time. Abigail and Adams worried endlessly over Nabby's marital problems. "My children give me more Pain than all my Ennemies," Adams complained in a letter to his wife.

John Adams had hoped to return to his law practice, but that proved to be impossible. He suffered from palsy, a disease that caused his hands to tremble. Speaking was also difficult, because most of his teeth had had to be extracted.

Neverthless, he was still able to enjoy the farming chores he had missed while away from home. He and Abigail found peace and contentment in ordinary activities. Abigail would rise early to skim the milk. She was often seen walking with her pet dog, Juno. "You will find your father in his fields," she wrote their son, "attending to his haymakers, and your mother busily occupied in . . . domestic concerns."

John and Abigail Adams enjoyed the companionship of family and old friends. Their son, Thomas, lived in the family home with his wife and child. John Quincy practiced law nearby in Boston and began a brilliant career in politics. He was elected as a congressman and then senator from Massachusetts. John Adams also continued his lifelong habit of letter writing. He corresponded with many interesting and important people. He rekindled his friendship with Thomas Jefferson. They wrote frequently comparing ideas on political, philosophical, and social subjects. Adams also worked on his autobiography. It was published in 1850, many years after his death, by his grandson, Charles Francis Adams.

Abigail Adams, "Dearest Friend"

John Adams might not have been John Adams without Abigail. He needed her support to accomplish the great things that he did for his country. Theirs was a remarkable partnership. They were equals in every way and shared equally in every important domestic decision. Abigail was just as dedicated as Adams to the great cause to which they both devoted their lives. She was willing to sacrifice her personal comfort and safety for the good of the country.

Adams was away from their home in Massachusetts for long periods of time. Abigail had the complete responsibility of running a home, raising children, and managing the business of their farm. She accepted this enormous burden as her contribution to the revolutionary effort. She performed the duties of a man as well as those that were expected of women. She brought to all her endeavors an enormous intelligence, as well as a determination to work hard and do whatever might be needed to reach her goals. She faced the trials of childbirth, war, death, and deprivation, mostly without her husband's presence or help.

Despite her overwhelming duties, Abigail somehow found the time to correspond regularly and in great detail. The letters that Adams and Abigail wrote offer a fascinating glimpse into their personal lives, as well as into the dramatic events of the period. They addressed each other as "Dearest Friend," and shared their thoughts on everything.

Abigail also wrote to Adams with important advice. All through war, politics, and nation building, she was his chief consultant and adviser. He relied on her understanding of complicated issues to help him with important decisions. When Adams was president, Abigail's opinions and suggestions carried more weight than those of his cabinet. During the second presidential campaign, she acted in the role of a campaign manager.

On their eighteenth anniversary, Adams wrote to Abigail that their love "burns with unabating fervor." It continued to burn through all the days of their lives.

Abigail continued to ail. She became more and more frail. Her husband, however, enjoyed good health for many years. He took long horseback rides and walked four miles a day. The Adamses received a blow in 1811 when Nabby was diagnosed with breast cancer. Surgery was performed without anesthesia, and she suffered horrible pain. Adams and Abigail cared for her, and she seemed to recover. But the cancer returned, and in 1813, Nabby died in her parents' arms.

Abigail continued to weaken too. In the fall of 1818, she fell ill with typhoid fever and died. She was seventy-four years old. She and Adams had been married for fifty-four years. John Adams was grief stricken at the loss of his beloved life partner. He saw only "desolation and solitude" ahead for himself. His physical condition began to deteriorate. But he remained alert and quick of mind.

John Adams had one more great triumph in his life. In 1825 his son John Quincy Adams was inaugurated as the sixth president of the United States. "The multitude of my thoughts, and the intensity of my feelings are too much for a mind like mine, in its ninetieth year,"

✧ ————————————

This portrait was painted in 1826, when Adams was ninety years old.

he wrote to his son. Adams was too weak to attend the inauguration, but the occasion brought him great joy and pride.

The year 1826 marked the fiftieth anniversary of the signing of the Declaration of Independence. John Adams was failing rapidly, but he was determined to live to see that glorious day. When asked to contribute a message to the celebration in Quincy, he told them, "I will give you Independence Forever." As the sun set on July 4, 1826, John Adams, American patriot, drew his last breath and died.

John Adams left an enduring legacy. The Founding Fathers of the American republic were all great and far-sighted men. Adams holds a place of honor within that remarkable group. He was hardworking and ambitious. His brilliant arguments, based on a deep understanding of history and law, gave moral and legal weight to the demands of the patriots. They are the basis for the American form of government that still exists.

John Adams had minor flaws such as a tendency to talk too much and to appear somewhat pompous to people who did not know him well. He was also easily hurt by criticism. However, he had a deep capacity for love and devotion to his wife, children, many friends, and country. He sacrificed his personal and family life so that the generations that followed could live in freedom.

THE ADAMS FAMILY

John and Abigail Adams were remarkable people. The family dynasty they started produced a number of exceptional men and women. Some of their well-known descendants included:

John Quincy Adams (1767–1848): At the age of fourteen, John Quincy *(left)* was appointed secretary to Francis Dana, minister to Russia. He accompanied Dana to Saint Petersburg, where he continued his studies. By then he knew Latin and Greek and could speak French, Dutch, and German. He later studied law at Harvard. Upon graduation he began a .successful law practice in Boston. In 1794 President George Washington appointed John Quincy minister to the Netherlands and then sent him to London. In London John Quincy met and married Louisa Catherine Johnson. Their marriage lasted fifty years, and they had four children. Back in Boston, John Quincy was elected to the U.S. Senate from Massachusetts. He served as secretary of state to President James Monroe. In 1825 John Quincy Adams became the sixth president of the United States. After his presidency, he represented Massachusetts in the U.S. House of Representatives from 1831 until his death.

Charles Francis Adams (1807–1886): Charles Francis Adams *(facing page, top)* was the third son of John Quincy. His grandmother, Abigail, called him "a thinking boy," and Charles

Francis worked hard to live up to the standards set by his parents and grandparents. He followed the family tradition of studying law at Harvard and entered public service. He married Abigail Brooks, and they had six children. Charles Francis served in the Massachusetts House of Representatives, the state senate, and the U.S. Congress. In 1861 he became a popular and effective diplomat, serving as minister to Britain for seven years.

Charles Francis used his outstanding writing and editing skills to obtain publication of the autobiographies of his father, John Quincy, and his grandfather, John Adams.

Henry Adams (1838–1918): Henry Adams *(below)* was the son of Charles Francis. Like the men in the earlier generations, Henry graduated from Harvard. His talents and interests were not in politics but in literature and history.

He served as an assistant professor of history at Harvard and was editor of an influential journal called the *North American Review.* He became well known as a historian and published many books, including *History of the United States during the Administrations of Thomas Jefferson* and *James Madison* and *Historical Essays.* His best known book is *The Education of Henry Adams.* It was popular in its time and is still read.

TIMELINE

1735   John Adams is born in Braintree (later Quincy), Massachusetts, on October 19.

1755   Adams graduates from Harvard and becomes a schoolmaster.

1758   Adams sets up a law practice in Braintree.

1764   Adams marries Abigail Smith on October 25.

1765   The Adamses' first daughter, Abigail (Nabby), is born. Great Britain imposes the Stamp Act on the colonies, and Adams joins the protest against it.

1767   The Adamses' first son, John Quincy, is born.

1768   The Adamses' second daughter, Susanna, is born. She dies two years later.

1770   The Boston Massacre occurs on March 5. Adams defends British soldiers in the Boston Massacre trial. The Adamses' second son, Charles, is born.

1772   The Adamses' third son, Thomas Boylston, is born.

1773   The Boston Tea Party occurs on December 16.

1774   Adams attends the First Continental Congress.

1775   The Battles of Lexington and Concord mark the start of the Revolutionary War. Adams attends the Second Continental Congress.

1776   Adams helps Thomas Jefferson draft the Declaration of Independence. Congress adopts the declaration on July 4.

1778   Adams sails to Paris with his oldest son, John Quincy, to become an American representative in France.

1779   Adams returns to America. He drafts the Massachusetts constitution. He returns to France with two of his sons.

1782   Adams negotiates a treaty of friendship with the Dutch. He helps negotiate the Treaty of Paris.

1784   Abigail and Nabby arrive in Europe.

1785   Adams serves as the first American ambassador to Great Britain until 1788. The Constitutional Convention is held in Philadelphia.

1788   Adams returns to the United States.

1789   Adams begins his first of two terms as the first vice president of the United States under President George Washington. He serves for eight years.

1797   Adams begins his four-year term as the second president of the United States. He appoints the first American peace comission to France. The scandal of the XYZ affair erupts.

1798   Adams signs the Alien and Sedition Acts, limiting free speech and public dissent.

1800   Adams signs a treaty with France, preventing war. He loses the next presidential election to Thomas Jefferson. His son Charles dies.

1801   Adams appoints several Supreme Court justices, including John Marshall, before his term as president ends. He retires to Quincy, leaving public life.

1813   The Adamses' daughter, Nabby, dies.

1818   Adams's wife, Abigail, dies.

1825   John Quincy Adams becomes the sixth president of the United States.

1826   John Adams dies on July 4, exactly fifty years after the adoption of the Declaration of Independence.

SOURCE NOTES

7 David McCullough, *John Adams* (New York: Simon & Schuster, 2001), 68.

8 James Bishop Peabody, ed., *John Adams: A Biography in His Own Words,* vol. 1 (New York: Newsweek, 1973), 118.

9 Peabody, 1: 20.

11 Jack Shepherd, *The Adams Chronicles* (Boston: Little Brown & Co., 1975), 4.

11 Page Smith, *John Adams,* vol. 1 (New York: Doubleday and Company, Inc., 1962), 11.

11 Ibid.

12 Ibid., 12.

12 Ibid.

12 Ibid., 13.

15 Catherine Drinker Bowen, *John Adams and the American Revolution* (Boston: Little Brown & Co., 1950), 140.

15 Smith, 1: 24.

15 Ibid., 25.

16 Ibid., 24.

16 Ibid., 25.

17 Shepherd, 8.

17 Smith, 1: 31.

17 Shepherd, 8.

18 Smith, 1: 33.

18 Ibid., 34.

18 Ibid.

18 Peabody, 1: 43.

19 Shepherd, 15.

19 Peabody, 1: 49.

19 Ibid., 49.

20 Smith, 1: 45.

21 Bowen, 225.

23 McCullough, 57.

25 Peabody, 1: 88.

25 Shepherd, 19.

25 Smith, 1: 64.

25 Peabody, 1: 87.

25 A. J. Langguth, *Patriots: The Men Who Started the American Revolution* (New York: Touchstone, 1988), 147.

25 Ibid.

29 Peabody, 1: 96.

31 Shepherd, 30.

31 Ibid.

32 Peabody, 1: 168.

35 Langguth, 96.

36 Ibid., 101.

36 Shepherd, 35.

36 Smith, 1: 99.

36 Bowen, 318.

37 Peabody, 1: 74.

37 Shepherd, 37.

37–38 Ibid., 38.

39 Smith, 1: 129.

39 Ibid., 130.

40 Ibid., 133.

40 Ibid., 134.

40 Ibid., 138.

40 Ibid., 138–139.

41 Ibid., 148.

42 Henry Wadsworth Longfellow, "Paul Revere's Ride," *Oxford Anthology of American Literature,* ed. William Rose Benet (New York: Oxford University Press, 1947), 576.

43 Shepherd, 52.

43 Langguth, 179.

43 Ibid.

43 Ibid.

44 Ibid., 181.

44 Ibid., 184.

44–45 Shepherd, 52–53.

45 Peabody, 1: 17.

46 Ibid., 150.

47 Smith, 1: 176.

49 Shepherd, 61.

50 Richard C. Wade, Howard B. Wilder, and Louise C. Wade, *A History of the United States* (Boston: Houghton Mifflin Co., 1972), 97–99.

50 Shepherd, 61.
51 Ibid., 64.
51–52 Ibid., 65.
52 Ibid.
53 Ibid., 67.
53 Ibid., 68.
54 Ibid.
54 Smith, 1: 222.
54 Ibid., 261.
55 Ibid., 271.
56 Shepherd, 76.
56 Ibid, 77.
56 Ibid.
56–57 Shepherd, 83.
57 Langguth, 360.
59 Smith, 1: 331.
59 Ibid., 333.
59 Shepherd, 87.
60 Ibid.
61 Smith, 1: 359.
62 McCullough, 192.
62 Shepherd, 89.
64 Ibid., 92.
64 Ibid.
65 Smith, 1: 450.
66 Shepherd, 100.
70 Smith, 1: 580.
70–71 Shepherd, 117.
71 Ibid., 116.
72 Page Smith, *John Adams,* vol. 2 (New York: Doubleday and Company, Inc., 1962), 625.
73 Shepherd, 118.
73 Ibid., 120.
74 Shepherd, 120.
75 Ibid., 121.
75 Ibid., 123.
76 Smith, 2: 654.
77 Shepherd, 127.
80 McCullough, 409.
83 Shepherd, 157.
83 Ibid., 159.
83 Ibid., 157.
83 Ibid., 159.
86 Smith, 2: 844.
86 Ibid, 880.
86 James Bishop Peabody, ed., *John Adams: A Biography in His Own Words,* vol. 2 (New York: Newsweek, 1973), 358.
86 Smith, 2: 917.
87 McCullough, 470.
87 Shepherd, 180.
88 McCullough, 526–527.
91 Shepherd, 202.
91 Ibid., 198.
91–92 Ibid.
93 Ibid., 210.
94 Ibid.
94 Ibid., 209.
95 Shepherd, 165.
95 Smith, 2: 1104.
95 Shepherd, 295.
96 McCullough, 647.
97 John Ferling, *John Adams: A Life* (New York: Henry Holt, 1992), 388.
97 Shepherd, 220.
99 Peabody, 2: 292.
100 Smith, 2: 1123.
100 Peabody, 2: 406.
101 McCullough, 645.
102 Shepherd, 271.

SELECTED BIBLIOGRAPHY

Adams, James Truslow. *The Adams Family.* New York: The Literary Guild, 1930.

Bowen, Catherine Drinker. *John Adams and the American Revolution.* Boston: Little Brown & Co., 1950.

Ellis, Joseph J. *Founding Brothers.* New York: Alfred A. Knopf, 2000.

Ferling, John. *John Adams: A Life.* New York: Henry Holt, 1992.

Langguth, A. J. *Patriots: The Men Who Started the American Revolution.* New York: Touchstone, 1988.

Lorant, Stefan. *The Glorious Burden.* Lenox, MA: Authors Edition, 1976.

McCullough, David. *John Adams.* New York: Simon & Schuster, 2001.

Morris, Juddi. At Home with the Presidents. New York: John Wiley & Sons, 1999.

Peabody, James Bishop, ed. *John Adams, A Biography in His Own Words.* 2 vols. New York: Newsweek, 1973.

Shepherd, Jack. *The Adams Chronicles.* Boston: Little Brown & Co., 1975.

Smith, Page. *John Adams.* 2 vols. New York: Doubleday and Company, Inc., 1962.

Zall, Paul M., ed. *The Wit & Wisdom of the Founding Fathers.* Hopewell, NJ: Ecco Press, 1996.

FURTHER READING AND WEBSITES

Adams National Historic Park. <http://www.nps.gov/adam/>. A travel guide to the fourteen-acre park, this site lists historic features as well as upcoming scheduled activities.

Adams Papers. <http://www.masshist.org/adams.html>. The Adams Papers Collection contains family letters, diaries, and manuscripts. The website includes selected documents, timelines, and quotations.

Beller, Susan Provost. *The Revolutionary War.* New York: Benchmark Books, 2002.

Bjornlund, Lydia D. *The Constitution and the Founding of America.* San Diego: Lucent, 1999.

Bohannon, Lisa Frederiksen. *The American Revolution.* Minneapolis: Lerner Publications Company, 2004.

Boston Massacre Trials 1770. <http://www.law.umkc.edu/faculty/ projects/ftrials/bostonmassacre/bostonmassacre.html>. This site is home to documents and images surrounding the Boston Massacre Trials. Read the words of eyewitnesses, the arguments of the lawyers, and a summary of the trial penned by John Adams.

Constitution of Massachusetts 1780. <http://www.nhinet.org/ccs/ docs/ma-1780.htm>. Investigate the rights and laws of Adams's home state. The constitution of Massachusetts is presented here in its original language and form.

Day, Nancy. *Your Travel Guide to Colonial America.* Minneapolis: Runestone Press, 2001.

Ferris, Jeri Chase. *Remember the Ladies: A Story about Abigail Adams.* Minneapolis: Carolrhoda Books, Inc., 2001.

Fradin, Dennis Brindell. *Samuel Adams: The Father of American Independence.* New York: Clarion Books, 1998.

Gaines, Ann Graham. *John Hancock: President of the Continental Congress.* Philadelphia: Chelsea House, 2001.

Hull, Mary E. *The Boston Tea Party in American History.* Berkeley Heights, NJ: Enslow Publishers, 1999.

Jones, Veda Boyd. *Alexander Hamilton: First U.S. Secretary of the Treasury.* Philadelphia: Chelsea House, 2000.

St. George, Judith. *John and Abigail Adams: An American Love Story.* New York: Holiday House, 2001.

Streissguth, Tom. *Benjamin Franklin.* Minneapolis: Lerner Publications Company, 2002.

Whitelaw, Nancy. *Thomas Jefferson: President and Philosopher.* Greensboro, NC: Morgan Reynolds, 2001.

INDEX

ABOUT THE AUTHOR

Carol H. Behrman was born in Brooklyn, New York, graduated from City College of New York, and attended Columbia University's Teachers' College, where she majored in education. For many years, Behrman taught grades five through eight at the Glen Ridge Middle School in New Jersey. She has written twenty books, fiction and nonfiction, for children and young adults, as well as five writing textbooks. Her previous biographies include *Fiddler to the World: The Inspiring Life of Itzhak Perlman, Roberto Clemente, Andrew Jackson,* and *Miss Dr. Lucy,* the story of the first woman dentist in America. Behrman lives in Sarasota, Florida.